NO LONGER PROPERTY OF
SEATTLE PUBLIC LIBRARY

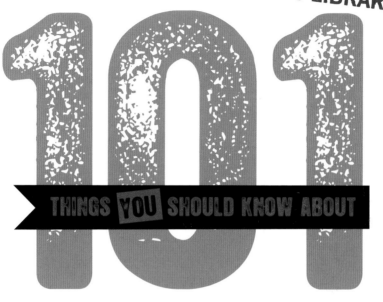

101

THINGS **YOU** SHOULD KNOW ABOUT

SOCIAL
STUDIES

D1041159

STERLING

New York

An Imprint of Sterling Publishing
387 Part Avenue South
New York, NY 10016

STERLING and the distinctive Sterling logo are
registered trademarks of Sterling Publishing Co., Inc.

Copyright © 2014 Pulp Media Limited

All rights reserved. No part of this publication may be reproduced,
stored in a retrieval system, or transmitted in any form or by any means (including
electronic, mechanical, photocopying, recording, or otherwise) without prior written
permission from the publisher.

ISBN 978-1-4549-1046-6

Distributed in Canada by Sterling Publishing
c/o Canadian Manda Group, 165 Dufferin Street
Toronto, Ontario, Canada M6K 3H6
Distributed in the United Kingdom by GMC Distribution Services
Castle Place, 166 High Street, Lewes, East Sussex, England BN7 1XU
Distributed in Australia by Capricorn Link (Australia) Pty. Ltd.
P.O. Box 704, Windsor, NSW 2756, Australia

For information about custom editions, special sales, and premium and corporate
purchases, please contact Sterling Special Sales at 800-805-5489 or
specialsales@sterlingpublishing.com.

For Pulp Media Limited:
AUTHOR: Sonia Mehta (in association with Quadrum Solutions)
SERIES ART DIRECTOR: Allen Boe
SERIES EDITOR: Helena Caldon
DESIGN & EDITING: Quadrum Solutions
PUBLISHER: James Tavendale

IMAGES courtesy of www.shutterstock.com

Manufactured in China

2 4 6 8 10 9 7 5 3 1

www.sterlingpublishing.com

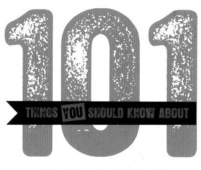

101
THINGS YOU SHOULD KNOW ABOUT

SOCIAL STUDIES

STERLING
New York

5

INTRODUCTION

7

HISTORY OF THE WORLD

29

ANCIENT CIVILIZATIONS

63

ANTHROPOLOGY

91

THE STUDY OF POLITICS

133

PSYCHOLOGY

143

SOCIOLOGY

185

ECONOMICS

INTRODUCTION

Once you go beyond your textbook filled with dates and names, Social Studies can be really interesting. For example, we bet you didn't know that Hobbit-like creatures actually roamed the Earth a couple of million years ago. Perhaps what J.R.R. Tolkien wrote in Lord of the Rings wasn't purely imagination. How do we know? By peeking into the evolution of man that proved the existence of such pint-sized humans called Homo floresiensis. Of course, it's hardcore history that takes us back in time to when we had just begun.

Social Studies deals with other interesting stuff too. There are many other topics that come under this fascinating umbrella, such as the way humans interact with each other, how countries go to war, plagues that brought the Earth to a standstill for a while, and the way humans deal with their cash. Open the book to find facts that will blow your mind and completely transform the way you look at Social Studies.

So if you've got a moment, settle down and take a look at how man evolved and where he has reached today.

EVOLUTION

LANGUAGE

COMMUNICATION

SURVIVAL OF THE FITTEST

STONE AGE

MIGRATION

IRON AGE

TOOLS

BRONZE AGE   NATURAL SELECTION

AUSTRALOPITHECUS

HISTORY OF THE WORLD

PILLOW

LAUGHTER

HOMO FLORESIENSIS   NOMAD

1. NATURAL SELECTION

Every living organism has a process called "natural selection" to thank for its existence. According to this process, Nature ensures that only those organisms which are best suited for their environment, or are the "fittest," survive. In this way, every species existing today has, at some point of time or the other, proven that it is "fitter" for survival than other species.

According to this theory, a long time ago, even before the dinosaurs, all forms of life lived underwater and the only vertebrates were fish. Obviously, at one point in time, there were a lot more fish than food and a lot of underwater competition for food.

This is where the strange story of evolution begins. Certain fish underwent mutation and developed muscles that helped

them push themselves up onto the land, which opened up a whole new world for them filled with delicious food! It is these mutated fish that went on to become the ancestors of the vertebrae that live on the land. If we go by this theory, we've descended from fish!

Hence, through natural selection, nature selected the fish that got mutated with the superpower of survival. This is the basis of evolution. Mutations that help the organism survive better in nature are selected and strengthened. This is what leads to the changing of species. If the conditions are conducive, with the right combinations of mutations, we may actually have a Spiderman or a Batman!

FAST FACT . . .
A cross between two species usually results in a DNA change.

FAST FACT . . .
Natural resources such as water and air are limited in the world. That's why, with the help of "natural selection," nature tries to maintain the balance in the population of living animals and plants in the world.

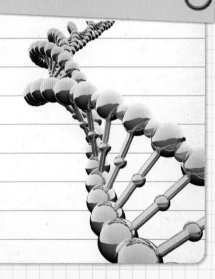

2. LAUGHTER

We've heard several times that laughter is the best medicine, but little do we know precisely how old this medicine is. There are a few things about laughter that are guaranteed to bring a smile to your lips.

We started laughing around seven million years ago – when we had not even begun to evolve as humans! Laughter is that old. Initially, laughter was involuntary; we didn't have control over our facial muscles. We cracked up every time we sensed that there was no danger and we could relax.

Over the years, humans gained control over their facial muscles. This caused the frequency of our laughter to decline.

Another interesting observation about laughter is that it is a contagious phenomenon. If one person begins to laugh out loud in a room full of solemn faces, slowly every face starts breaking into a smile and then begins to laugh. Looks like yawning isn't the only contagious phenomenon!

One such instance – a laughter epidemic – broke out in Tanzania in 1962, a few weeks after the nation gained independence. A little girl began giggling, because the tiny village was relieved. People slowly started joining in and began to laugh. Back then, there were around 10,000 people laughing at the same time!

FAST FACT . . .
Statistics suggest that women laugh more than men.

FAST FACT . . .
Chimpanzees have been known to laugh during their tumble plays.

3. THE FIRST HUMANS

Around 2.5 million years ago, a bunch of our ancestors, called the "Australopithecus," found a warm and cozy zone on the southern coast of Africa to settle down. These were the first humans to inhabit the world.

When Homo Sapiens began to evolve, Earth was going through one of its cold spells, or ice ages. This made it too cold for human beings to live anywhere else. In this icy cold weather, the warm and cozy setting on the southern coast of Africa was the perfect place for humans to live in. That is how this area became the first dwelling of our human ancestors.

This was the era of the Stone Age. It was a time when humans used stones for hunting. The Stone Age went on for more than a million years, and it was only 200,000 years ago that man began to make more sophisticated tools.

Humans lived in close proximity to animals, and had to live in groups to keep safe. It is strange to imagine that the organized, sophisticated societies that we live in today actually descended from animalistic herds that stuck together for hunting and survival.

Since primitive humans lived close to the sea near the southern tip of Africa, shellfish was their staple diet.

FAST FACT . . .

It is believed that while men in the Stone Age probably traveled in hunting packs or groups into the mainland in search of food, women mostly stayed near the coast.

FAST FACT . . .

While the favorite non-vegetarian diet of those times consisted of livers, kidneys, and other internal organs of animals that humans hunted, the vegetarian diet included leaves, roots, and wild cereal grains.

4. STONE TOOLS

These were the first tools used by man. They marked the Stone Age, which went on from 2.5 million years ago till about 20,000 years ago, which means that it lasted for more than 2 million years! During those long years, man learnt to carve various kinds of stone tools that helped him hunt.

The Stone Age is divided into the Paleolithic Era and the Neolithic Era. The Paleolithic Era is the Old Stone Age, while the Neolithic Era is the New Stone Age. During these ages, man used stone to hunt, carve the hunted meat, and grow crops.

Some of the tools that came to be used in this era were spearheads, flints, and hand axes. The need to make such tools arose because man's hands were not strong enough for hunting or digging the ground.

What differentiated human beings from other animals was our possession of opposable thumbs; having these meant that our thumbs could move in different directions from the rest of our fingers, which gave us the ability to grasp objects and handle tools, unlike other animals. Press your thumbs against the forefingers on the same hand. This tiny motion is the reason why you can write and your pet dog can't.

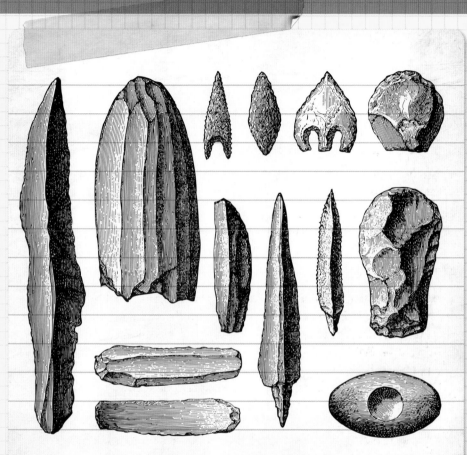

FAST FACT . . .

Apart from stones, humans had also started using bones and wood as tools during the Stone Age.

5. THE THREE AGES

The history of mankind can be divided into three ages – the Stone Age, the Bronze Age, and the Iron Age. Man created these divisions based on the material that was most extensively used during that era.

The Stone Age

The Stone Age began about 2.5 million years ago, when man first started settling on the southern shores of Africa. Man started using large stones to hunt. Slowly, he began shaping these stones in order to use them in a more efficient manner. The Stone Age is further divided into three eras. The Old Stone Age is known as the Paleolithic era. This was when man used stones in their original form for hunting.

After this era, man started focusing on the details of the stone. Large weapons slowly began to shrink in size. This was

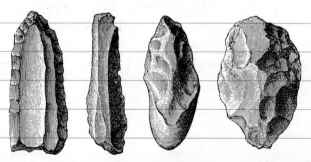

Tools from the Stone Age

FAST FACT . . .
A lot of what we now know about the Stone Age has been found out by carefully examining the caves in which the people of that age lived.

A kettle from the Bronze Age

the Middle Stone Age, or the Mesolithic era. The last era of the Stone Age was the Neolithic era during which man took to agriculture. He began growing his own food.

The Bronze Age

The Bronze Age began around 3000 B.C., when man first stumbled upon the technology of smelting ores in Southwest Asia. He discovered that the Earth contains a shiny metal which can be used to make weapons and ornaments. First, man discovered copper. Then, he mixed copper with zinc and got a metal called bronze, which was more useful than copper.

The Iron Age

The Iron Age also began in Southwest Asia, in about 1000 B.C. The discovery of iron led to a revolution in mankind. This revolution hasn't ended yet. We are technically still living in the Iron Age!

6. HOMO FLORESIENSIS

Hobbits inhabited not only the Middle Earth, but this very Earth too! So, if you thought Hobbits only resided in J.R.R. Tolkien's imagination, you are mistaken. Around 18,000 years ago, on the island of Flores in Indonesia, lived people who were one-third the size of human beings.

These mini-humans were a species that were called the Homo floresiensis. When archeologists in Indonesia came across the miniature skull of a woman among many others, they were reminded of these mythical creatures that, till then, had resided only in J.R.R. Tolkien's mind.

The question now is, how could an entire population of hobbit-like creatures vanish? Though there are several theories that explain the cause of their disappearance, the reason is not yet clearly known. Some scientists believe that Homo sapiens (human beings in their current form) adapted better to that environment. Since Homo floresiensis could not adapt as well, they were eliminated by the process of natural selection. In other words, we were "fitter" than the Homo floresiensis (remember the theory of the survival of the fittest discussed earlier?). Another group of scientists believe that a volcanic eruption – CampiFalgrei – led to their extinction.

FAST FACT . . .

The wrists of these Hobbit-like beings weren't as well-developed as those of their human counterparts, which is why they couldn't lift heavy objects. This could have played a role in their extinction.

7. PILLOWS

You thought pillows are a modern luxury, didn't you? If you did, you couldn't be more wrong! People from ancient civilizations were well aware of the comfort a raised head offered while sleeping, but their pillows were a bit different from ours.

The earliest pillow discovered by archeologists dates back to 7000 B.C. It was found in Mesopotamia, which is located in modern-day Iraq. This pillow was a block of stone with a slightly curved top to pose as a headrest. The ancestor of the modern pillow can be traced back to Mesopotamian blocks of stone.

What's more, Ancient Egyptians also liked to have a pillow under their heads as they slept. It is believed that the Egyptians began using pillows in order to prevent insects and other bugs from crawling into their ears, mouth and nose while they were sleeping. However, though the luxury of soft, cushy pillows did exist at that time in Ancient Egypt, they were almost never used. Even though the Egyptians had a comfy pillow, they preferred to lean their heads against stone blocks while sleeping. Strange, isn't it? Let's hope that someday, the logic behind these stone pillows becomes clear, but until then, count your blessings every time you sleep on a pillow that is not made of stone!

FAST FACT . . .

The Egyptians weren't the only ones to enjoy a hard pillow. The ancient Chinese and Japanese, too, preferred sleeping on hard pillows. The Ancient Greeks and Romans, on the other hand, used soft pillows made of cloth and stuffed with feathers, reeds, or straw.

FAST FACT . . .

Five centuries ago, Confucius said about the pillow: "With coarse rice to eat, with water to drink, and my bended arm for a pillow – I have still joy in the midst of these things."

8. NOMADIC HUNTERS

Nomadic hunters came to North America from as far as Asia, on foot. Ancient man walked and walked in search of food and adventure and crossed the Bering Land Bridge that once connected the two continents. Finally, Man arrived on the American sub-continent. This was the beginning of life in America.

This mega marathon walk took place at the end of the last Ice Age, some 15,000 years ago. Strange as it is to believe, this still meant that America was the second-last continent to become inhabited by man.

(Antarctica remains the last). What took Man so long to discover this continent? Many researchers have pondered upon this question, and the consensus seems to be that the main culprit is ice.

Until the end of the last Ice Age, most of the route leading to America was still covered with ice. Even though Man had become accustomed to hunting and residing in such extreme conditions, there was little he could do when he was confronted with huge blocks of ice.

As the last Ice Age came to an end, the ice on the path leading to America began to melt. Slowly, Man started walking towards America. Going by this route, man first inhabited North America and then moved to South America.

FAST FACT . . .

The oldest human remains in America have been found in the Fishbone Cave in western Nevada, Arlington Springs, on Santa Rosa Islands and, the Anzick site in Montana.

FAST FACT . . .

The age of fossils can be determined with the help of radiocarbon dating.

9. ORIGIN OF LANGUAGE

Animals around us don't really talk, but they sure do communicate. This was the case with human beings too. When Man lived in the wild, not in societies, but in herds, and went hunting with fellow humans, he felt the need to communicate. That's how the story of language began.

A long time ago, during the Stone Age, man often went out on hunting expeditions in groups. If one man was busy fishing, and another spotted a fish, he would want to inform the first guy about the good news and also ask for his help in hunting it. It was then that he realized he couldn't call the other man, because there was no language, so he waved, then grunted, and made funny gestures. Of course, the noise probably scared all the fish away, but man discovered that there was a chance he could convey his message to other people. After that, largely through trial and error, man began to standardize this way of communication. He started using various sounds, hoots, claps, and howls to convey particular ideas and emotions. Another factor that lead to the development of our sophisticated means of communication was the fact that, as a species, we began to stand erect. This led to alterations in our vocal cords and made voice modulation possible for us.

FAST FACT . . .

The area in the brain which buzzes with activity as far as language is concerned is the "Wernicke's Area."

10. EVOLUTION ACCELERATION

We have now pieced together the story of human evolution and can clearly see the changes that the human race has gone through since the Stone Age. That's because we can now look back, study millions of years of information, and see a clear picture. But could it be that evolution is still an ongoing process? We don't seem to be changing size or shape or growing extra limbs. Does that mean we aren't evolving any more?

In fact, the evidence is quite to the contrary, pointing towards an accelerated rate of evolution. We're just unable to notice these changes because of how gradual they are. Almost 10,000 years is, in the history of humans, a very short span of time. Because we're living through this rapid phase of evolution, we aren't really able to see it.

Even so, scientists who have been collecting data over the years have concluded that we are indeed evolving, and at a very rapid rate. Some major changes in our DNA have taken place in the last 200 generations. This has been determined by looking at the number of mutations that have taken place.

FAST FACT . . .

While "natural selection" has weakened, "random selection" has grown stronger.

Changes in the DNA transform into a perceptible change in body only after thousands of years, and after being tested by the all-time-favorite, very popular method of nature i.e.,"natural selection."

The catch here is that nature wasn't expecting us to evolve so soon, and so the process of "natural selection" just got a little delayed.

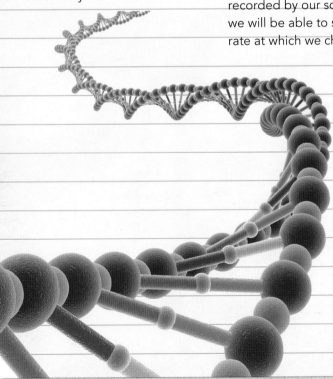

FAST FACT . . .

73 percent of genetic variation has been credited to the last 5,000 years.

When we look back into our history 10,000 years down the line and go through the data recorded by our scientists today, we will be able to see the quick rate at which we changed.

MESOPOTAMIA

SPARTA

CLEOPATRA

ANCIENT EGYPT

MAYANS

INDUS VALLEY CIVILIZATION

SENET

ZIGGURAT

PHARAOH

MAYAN

HAZDA

WHEEL

ANCIENT CIVILIZATIONS

HIEROGLYPHICS

AZTECS

ENGLISH LANGUAGE

11. ZIGGURATS

One of the earliest known civilizations resided in Mesopotamia. It is situated in present-day Iraq and is known as the "cradle of civilization." This is because all the first inventions were made here, including the wheel, one of the greatest inventions by mankind.

The land between the Rivers Tigris and Euphrates is known as Mesopotamia. This was where man first started farming and agriculture. It was easiest to begin in this part of the world because of the ready availability of water from both the rivers. Along with agriculture, the Mesopotamians also started building a very primitive kind of society. Around 3500 B.C., the

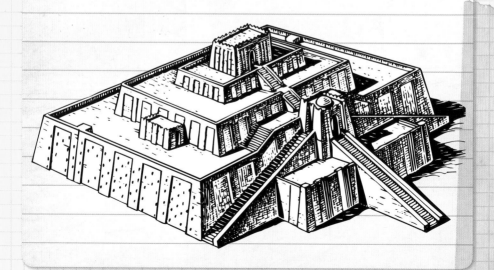

first cities of the world – Ur, Uruk, and Eridu – came into being in Mesopotamia. Along with that came a host of simple rituals and traditions.

This led to the creation of the Ziggurats, or the "holy mountains," where people went to pray, which were usually built on raised land with the help of bricks and mud.

In the ancient days, temples were places of prime importance, so vital decisions regarding trade and politics were taken at the temple by the priests. In those days, priests were considered to be no less than gods.

FAST FACT . . .
The Sumerians in Mesopotamia were the first to form an urban society.

FAST FACT . . .
The Ziggurat, situated in Ur, which is modern-day Iran, was built in 2100 B.C.

12. SPARTA

The Spartans were very particular about physical fitness. After all, in those days winning a war was more necessary than writing literature or trying to figure out what lay in outer space. Hence, it was no wonder that physical prowess was valued over everything else. The Spartans left no stones unturned to ensure that only the fittest survived.

To make sure that the State constantly consisted of only the strongest, fittest citizens, all newborn children were presented to a council of ministers. These ministers checked the babies for any physical defect or deformity. If the baby was found to be unfit, it was abandoned by the State. As shocking as it sounds, historians do believe that it's true.

FAST FACT . . .
Children were sent away for military training at the young age of seven in Sparta.

FAST FACT . . .

Spartan men had only one occupation by default – that of a soldier – and they served the country till the age of 60.

A lot of the babies who were abandoned by the hillside were later rescued and brought up by strangers, though.

The ordeal of being born a Spartan child didn't end there! Babies who did pass this first test of physical perfection were further tested by being bathed in wine and then left alone in the dark. Spartan babies were expected to be fearless and strong enough to fight against diseases.

Even when they cried, they were often ignored by their parents, because it was thought that this would make them tougher.

Another gory Spartan practice was called the "contest of endurance." Once a year, all the teenage Spartans were publicly beaten, sometimes till they died. It was thought to be a religious ritual as well as a way to test the boys' bravery and resistance to pain.
Only those who passed all these tough tests were deemed worthy enough of being a Spartan.

13. CLEOPATRA

We all know that Cleopatra was the last reigning queen of the Pharaohland of Egypt, but very few are aware that she wasn't actually born Egyptian. She was the last queen of Egypt, after which the State deteriorated. Cleopatra had held it all together as an ace politician.

Cleopatra was born in 69-68 B.C. into the Ptolemaic dynasty in Egypt. Her father, Ptolemy XII, died in 51 B.C., which was when Cleopatra was appointed as the heir to the throne along with her 10-year-old brother Ptolemy XIII. They were all descendants of the Macedonian Greeks, who were ruling Egypt during those times.

FAST FACT . . .
In Egypt, the Ptolemaic dynasty ruled from 323-30 B.C.

While it was common practice for the rulers of the Ptolemaic dynasty to follow the Greek culture, Cleopatra decided to set aside the Greek traditions and honor Egyptian traditions instead. She was the first Ptolemaic ruler who knew the Egyptian language.

A lot has been said about Cleopatra – her looks and her intelligence – and all the traits made her one of the most successful Queens or Kings. She is so deeply associated with Egypt and the Egyptian culture that it is no wonder that history often forgets to mention her lineage.

FAST FACT . . .
Cleopatra became queen at the age of 17.

FAST FACT . . .
While Cleopatra is popularly associated with beauty, historical evidence states that she actually had a crooked nose and masculine features.

14. EGYPTIAN BOARD GAMES

It's true that Egyptians did like their fair share of board games. In fact, it could be said that they loved their games to death – considering that board games have been recovered from the tombs of pharaohs. What games did they play? Scrabble? Monopoly? Not really! They had their own set of interesting games. Here's a peek.

As you sit contemplating your next move in chess, know that an Egyptian Pharaoh, several thousands of years ago, faced a similar dilemma. Pondering over the next move in a board game during long, idle hours was indeed on the to-do list of the Pharaohs.

However, the games they played differed from ours slightly. The most common game during those times was "Senet."

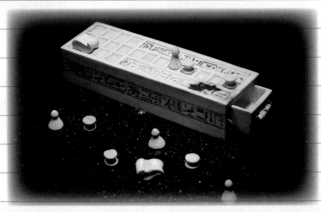

It was played by all, irrespective of their social strata. Some of these boards have survived with their counters and throw sticks. Unfortunately, the rules of the game are still unknown, though there have been attempts to reconstruct the game.

The board had 30 squares laid out in three rows of 10. Some of the squares had symbols on them and the path of the counters probably followed a reversed "S" across the board. The symbols represented either good or bad fortune, and affected the play accordingly. Instead of dice, this game was played with sticks, which were thrown to determine how many steps the player would move. It's somewhat similar to "Parcheesi," but more complicated. The board had a number of symbols that depicted good and bad luck, and the aim was to reach the destination without falling prey to most pitfalls. The person who managed to get all his pieces "Home" safely, won. Now we know what Pharaohs like Tutankhamen did in their free time!

FAST FACT . . .
Board games of Egypt are known be as ancient as 3500 B.C.

FAST FACT . . .
Apart from stones, Ancient Egyptian paintings reveal that Queen Nefertiti was also a fan of Senet.

15. POT-BELLIED PHARAOHS

Have you ever seen a mummy that points at the weight issues of a Pharaoh? Though this fact probably can't be attested till time travel is made possible, records about the royal diet of the kings and queens of those days suggest that there is a slight possibility that Pharaohs were overweight.

We have always believed that Pharaohs were lean and fit individuals, which makes this fact a little difficult to believe. We don't always associate pot bellies with the Egyptians, but after studying their royal diet – which mainly consisted of beer, wine, honey, and bread – historians are forced to conclude that, in reality, the Pharaohs may have looked a tad different from the images in our heads.

Confirming such suspicion is evidence that points in the direction of mummies that are inflicted with diabetes.

So it is more than likely that the Pharaohs were slightly on the heavier side. But they ensured that their tomb, mummies, and paintings didn't reflect their bulging waistline. After all, most of us would probably not like to be remembered that way.

FAST FACT . . .
There are also records that point towards arthritis being prevalent amongst the people of ancient Egypt.

FAST FACT . . .

Queen Hatshepsut is known to have been quite obese and balding. Her sarcophagus, though, shows her as a pretty, slim lady, with luscious flowing hair.

16. EGYPTIAN SNIFFER DOGS

We've all seen the famous sniffer dogs at crime scenes in detective shows on television, but did you know that this scene is not very different from what probably happened in ancient Egypt? In fact, the Egyptians were so fond of their pets that some of them have even found their way to their owner's tombs!

We've always associated cats with ancient Egyptian culture, but we haven't heard much about Egyptians keeping pet dogs. According to ancient Egyptian culture, quite a few animals were thought to symbolize revered gods and goddesses. To honor the heavenly beings, Egyptians kept pet animals at home.

Of course, it is a well-known fact that cats were their favorite pets, as these animals have made appearances in numerous paintings, tombs, and records.

Egyptians believe that the cat represented the goddess Bastet, who was responsible for protecting women. Other holy animals were dogs, ibises, hawks, lions, and baboons.

Ancient Egyptian dogs were used as guard dogs. Historians believe that they were even given collars. They often accompanied law enforcers and hunters of the time to keep an eye out for danger. It is thought that the dogs who usually accompanied ancient Egyptians were greyhounds, salukis, or dachshunds.

FAST FACT . . .
Ancient Egyptian word for dog was "iwiw."

17. THE MAYANS

Like all civilizations – ancient and modern – beauty played a major role in the life of the Mayans. However, the Mayans' perception of beauty was rather strange. They believed that cross-eyed children looked cuter than normal children, so they went that extra mile and made sure that their children's eyes crossed at a very young age!

In the sixth century A.D., the tropical lowlands of what is known as Guatemala today once came under the Mayan Empire. This civilization was Mesoamerican. It prided itself on its architecture, pottery, mathematics, calendar-making, and hieroglyphic writing. Even then, just as much attention was devoted to beauty as was to intellect, so the Mayans took utmost care that their citizens met all standards of beauty. The definition of beauty then was quite different.

Mayans considered a flat forehead and crossed eyes to be beautiful. Alas, not all children were blessed with such features, so many Mayans took it upon themselves to beautify their children.

How did they do it? In order to obtain cross-eyes, objects were dangled very close to an infant's eyes. This caused the child's eyes to cross, and gave the parents a reason to rejoice!

FAST FACT . . .

In order to flatten their children's foreheads, the Mayans resorted to pressing boards against that part of their child's head.

FAST FACT . . .

It's a well-known fact that the Mayans used to perform blood sacrifices to appease the Gods. However, not many people are aware that some of these rituals still continue. However, human blood has been replaced by chicken blood.

18. MAYAN SACRIFICE

The Mayans believed that you could attain enlightenment by jumping in water. Hold on before you go jumping into every puddle in sight, though, as no old puddle or well served as the magic portal to enlightenment. The Mayans had designated limestone sinkholes filled with water and believed that if you jumped into these, you would find enlightenment.

This is the story of human sacrifice in the Mayan civilization. The Mayans believed that jumping in these sinkholes – which they referred to as "cenotes" – would help one attain enlightenment. They believed that Chaak, the Rain God, resided in these cenotes.

FAST FACT . . .

Taking a sauna or a sweat-bath was a way of purification for Mayans.

Excavation at such sites has revealed a number of fractured skulls and other bones of people who presumably jumped in to search for the higher truth.

19. HADZA

The Hadza culture is found in Northern Tanzania around Lake Eyasi. Researchers have realized that their culture is quite different from others in the world. The Hadza people still depend on hunting and gathering for their sustenance. Even genetically, they are different from the rest of us, but what is strangest about these people is their language.

The Hadza tribe has remained unchanged for almost 10,000 years. The language of the Hadzabe people is called "Hadzane." It is made up of tongue clicks and plops and weird noises that are unlike any other modern language.

FAST FACT . . .

The Hadzane language is also known as the "click-language."

There are about 1,000–1,500 people who are a part of the Hadza tribe, and they live in camps. They know virtually nothing of the world beyond their direct existence!

20. THE ENGLISH SCRIPT

Have you ever wondered why Hebrew and Arabic is written from right to left, Chinese is written from top to bottom, and English from left to right? Technically, it's because the Greeks said so.

Ancient Greek scholars experimented by putting words on tablets in various ways before reading them. They found that going from left to right was the most convenient and easiest, so that's what they followed. Once the Greeks were conquered by the Romans, the Romans took on this practice too. Since Latin is the root of English and all other Western languages, English, French, German, and most other modern languages are written from the left to the right.

FAST FACT . . .

It was the Greeks who invented the amphitheater. You now know where all the drama began!

So, the only reason why you're reading this horizontally from the left to the right is because of the whim of some ancient Greek scholar!

21. THE WRITTEN WORD

The story of the written word begins from the
time of the cavemen. They started making
inscriptions on cave walls, scratching with
stone on the walls to express themselves.
It wasn't English, or even any particular
language that they scratched, but it began
with simple scratches and crosses.

In dark caves by the light of
the fire, cavemen first began to
paint things they saw around
them. After that, around
25,000 years ago, man started
developing symbols. He
designed a script that involved
26 characters, made up of dots,
dashes, squiggles, and many
other scratches.
Another amusing thing about
writing is the word itself.
The word "write" in Old English
means "scratch." The precise
Old English word for it was
"writan."
The term was coined when
writing was done with quill pens
on papyrus.

FAST FACT . . .
The word pen comes from
"penna," which means
feathers.

22. THE AZTECS

The Aztecs belonged to an ancient civilization that probably originated in Mexico. They lived in Mesoamerica in the 13th century. Although Aztecs are known largely as barbaric, unorganized warmongers, you'd be surprised to learn that the Aztecs were quite a complex community.

To begin with, the Aztecs had their own language – N'ahuatl– which was pictorial in nature. Since writing was something that needed specialized training in the Aztec society, it was limited to priests and scholars. Barks of trees and deer skins were used to record useful information like tax records and historical records.

The Aztecs were also very artistic people. They were into pottery, sculpting, and painting too! The most rampant form of art (in keeping with their barbaric stereotypes), though, was art designed for their warriors, which were then tattooed onto them as a mark of honor.

Another system that holds your attention is that of education. Education was necessary in the Aztec community, but there were separate schools for boys and girls and yet another one for the nobility. The education

FAST FACT . . .

The school dedicated to the children of nobility was called Calmecac school, while the one for the lower class was called Cuicacalli school.

provided in each differed according to class and gender.

The Aztecs were great warriors, and though it is popularly believed that the Spanish invasion led to the demise of these people, the truth is that the Spaniards were far behind the Aztecs when it came to warfare.

FAST FACT . . .
The education for girls focused on teaching them about domestic chores.

The end came for the Aztecs when they contracted smallpox, a European disease that wiped out a majority of its population.

23. INDUS VALLEY CIVILIZATION

In the 1920s, the Indus Valley was excavated and the world was exposed to this impressive ancient civilization. It was indeed a revelation because of the size, practices, and culture of the Indus Valley Civilization. Here's what so special about this ancient setting.

As Mesopotamia and Egypt developed in other parts of the world, a civilization was thriving in the Indus Valley during the Bronze Age. The Indus Valley Civilization was a civilization that developed around the River Indus sometime around 2300 B.C. It extended all the way from modern Pakistan to India. The most striking part about this civilization was its drainage system.

It was so well-planned and well-laid that even today engineers are in awe of it.

Apart from the drainage, even the cities were well-planned, with organized irrigation and plumbing facilities. Some of the most well-known structures of this civilization are Mohenjo-Daro, or the Great Bath, religious structures, and huge granaries which were located in the upper part of the dwelling. In the lower part was the residential area that was laid out neatly. Roads ran in perfect lines and were 30 meters in width.

FAST FACT . . .

People from Indus Valley Civilization worshipped animal forms.

The occupation of people here was usually farming or trading. It is believed that there were very minimalistic rules that divided the society. All were considered an equal here. Almost an ideal society, wasn't it?

FAST FACT . . .
The Indus Valley Civilization covered an area of about 486.5 miles.

The Indus Valley Civilization flourished for about 1,000 years and faded away. While some believe that a severe drought wiped out the state, others feel that Aryan invaders are to blame.

24. THE WHEEL

You may have often heard people refer to any great discovery or invention as being "the greatest invention since the wheel." Who invented the wheel? This accolade, along with the invention of many other "firsts," is credited to the Sumerians, who lived in Mesopotamia.

Mesopotamia was a civilization that was snugly settled in the middle of two rivers – the Tigris and the Euphrates. Since they were so close to all that water, the first invention of the Sumerians of Mesopotamia (not very surprisingly) was the sail-boat. This helped them to catch more fish and also helped in irrigation.

Of course, the other big invention, for which they are most famous, is the wheel. They first observed that they could move faster on a

FAST FACT . . .
The Sumerians were experts in metalwork. Their fame in this arena was known far and wide.

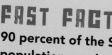

FAST FACT . . .
90 percent of the Sumerian population was involved in farming.

round log, and they began to experiment with other round objects. Finally, they got the hang of it and the wheel was invented. They used it for

FAST FACT . . .

The Sumerians traded through the Mediterranean route.

transporting heavy goods from one place to another.

The Sumerians were also the first to use a pictorial kind of writing, which was called "Cuneiforms." They made marks on the clay tablets with the help of a pointed reed called a "stylus," which is why the long pen-like device that accompanies touchscreen devices is also called a stylus.

25. EGYPTIAN HIEROGLYPHICS

While pictorial writing was still at its toddler stage, in all ancient civilizations of the world, Egypt was already acing in it. The ancient Egyptians had developed such an elaborate system of writing that Egyptologists took years to decipher the meanings behind the oh-so-many symbols.

All the monuments, tombs, and other stone structures in Egypt are peppered with hieroglyphics. It took Egyptologists many years to decipher the meaning of the symbols, because Egyptians didn't write in the same direction. They could either write from left to right or right to left. Sometimes, they even wrote from top to bottom. Also, there are no vowels in Egyptian writing, which was another cause for confusion among all the archeologists and Egyptologists.

Moreover, apart from these technical difficulties, there were more than 700 hieroglyphics to be deciphered. Phew! The symbols usually denoted birds, animals, and forces of nature. There were two kinds of hieroglyphics.

FAST FACT . . .
Most of the people in Egypt did not read or write. That's not a big surprise, considering the complexity of the language!

One was "Ideograms," where the symbol stood for the word; for example the drawing of man stood for the word "man." Then, there were phonograms, which represented the sound of the word they represented.

FAST FACT . . .

The Egyptians didn't use punctuations at all!

26. DREAM INTERPRETATION

Dreams take us into a whole other world.
Sometimes, they can be scary, other times
they can be utterly ridiculous and they make
us laugh. Today, though dreams are viewed
as an outlet of our subconscious thoughts,
dream interpretation is not given even half the
attention it was during ancient times.
Back then, dreams were viewed as hints from
another life or the afterlife.

What was so important about dream interpretation in the ancient days? Back then, a lot of importance was given to spirituality, so it was believed that dreams were a way to communicate with the spiritual self. The people of those cultures believed that dreams held the solution to many of their problems.

Dreams in those days were usually either simple or symbolic. Simple dreams involved the self and the usual mundane articles and activities that men of those times were surrounded by. Symbolic dreams, on the other hand, didn't make much sense. In order to get these dreams interpreted, people would seek the help of gods, priests, scholars, and dream interpreters. In Mesopotamia, it was believed that if you

FAST FACT . . .
We usually dream 1,460-2,190 dreams per year, though we usually remember only a fraction of these.

dreamed of anything evil, your entire body needed to be cleaned with the help of rituals. It was around 400 B.C. that Hippocrates, a Greek physician, suggested that dreams might be linked to certain psychological problems. For example, a dream about food could indicate that the person was suffering from some kind of depression.

FAST FACT . . .

By a method called "lucid dreaming," you can actually control your dreams!

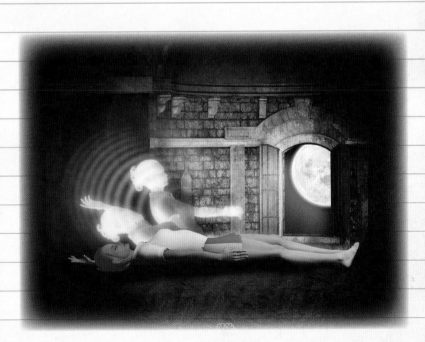

27. ORACULAR POWERS

An oracle was a way to foretell the future. The power to do this was vested in the priestess of Pythiaat who resided in the Temple of Apollo at Delphi. She sat on a tripod and inhaled ethylene gases. To listen to one's future outlined in such a way was a famous practice in ancient Greece.

The fame of Pythia spread in the eighth century, and the temple came to be known internationally as the location of the "Oracular Powers." All major decisions were taken only after consultation with Pythia. But how did it all work?

The Temple of Apollo was not open to the general public all the time, and a layman could visit the site only on a few select days.

FAST FACT . . .
A method of fortune telling, called "Geomancy," unravels clues about the future by listening to hysterical laughter.

People who were really in need of Pythia's fortune-telling skills paid huge amounts of money to find out what the future held in store for them.

FAST FACT . . .
Dreaming about an attic could mean that you need to renew an old friendship.

The priest of Pythia was Plutarch, and he revealed a great deal about the processes here. According to the sacred process, Pythia would enter the inner chamber of the temple, called Adyton, and inhale the ethylene gas escaping from the chasm of the Earth. This would send her into a state of trance. She would then begin muttering incoherently, and no one but the priest could understand what she was saying. The priest would then translate it for the layman.

28. THE COLOSSEUM

The enormous Colosseum has been the prime attraction in Rome since its construction. It was once the hub of entertainment, and people from all over Rome gathered in this amphitheater to cheer their favorite players in the ancient games that were played in the arena.

The Colosseum, which is about 620 by 513 feet in dimensions, was built in 80 A.D., but the permission to build the Colosseum was granted by Emperor Vespasian in 70-72 A.D. The generous emperor wanted to present this great entertainment hub to his people but he couldn't do the honors because of his age. So his son, Titus, completed this great architectural project and opened the gates of the Colosseum to the public in 80 A.D.

The Colosseum was officially known as the Flavian-amphitheater, and it was just like the stadiums we see today. Of course, there were no football or baseball matches in the Colosseum; the hot favorite games of those times were more barbaric in nature. The sports played in the Colosseum back then were gladiator combats, bull fights, and other such violent games.

FAST FACT . . .
The Colosseum is located in the east of the Roman Forum.

The public sat all around and cheered for their favorite player. This great amphitheater could accommodate around 50,000 spectators, who sat in specific seats according to their social ranking.

FAST FACT . . .
The Colosseum has about 80 entrances!

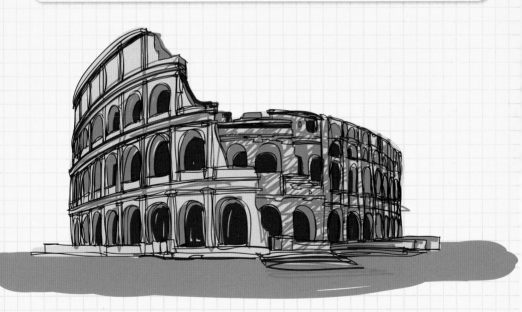

INDUSTRIAL REVOLUTION

MESOPOTAMIA

NEANDERTHALS

PASTORAL SOCIETIES

HUNTER-GATHERERS

EGALITARIAN

HORTICULTURAL SOCIETIES

STONE-AGE

AGRICULTURAL SOCIETIES

BARTER SYSTEM

VEGETARIANS

PASTORAL SOCIETIES

ANTHROPOLOGY

EMOTIONS

DEATH RITUALS

SHANIDAR

29. THE ORIGIN OF SHAVING

It's true that man started shaving way back in the Stone Age, but with the absence of the luxury that today's razors provide, the primitive method of shaving was rather painful. Around a million years ago, man first started pulling out his facial hair! Gradually, he learnt to use seashells as tweezers.

Once man evolved and ancient civilizations were formed, people started noticing their body hair. While there have been instances in the Stone Age where man has pulled out his facial hair, it wasn't a practice that was very regularly followed. It was more of a one-off thing. However, once civilizations developed and wars were fought, soldiers realized that facial hair could prove to be dangerous as it gives the enemy something to hold on to and pull. Thus began the practice of shaving.

Also, in the Ancient Egyptian culture, body hair was considered to be unkempt and barbaric. This was probably because of their hot climate, and the nuisance of lice.

Initially, man used flint stones for shaving, but slowly, as he evolved, he graduated to metals like copper, bronze, and iron, which gave rise to blades.

FAST FACT . . .
Egyptian women also used pumice stones and depilatory creams to get rid of their body hair.

FAST FACT . . .
Women started getting rid of body hair a long time after men did.

30. ANCESTRAL VEGETARIANS

In spite of living in the wild, research points at evidence that prehistoric man might, in fact, have been vegetarian. This means our ancestors inherently fed only on wild plants, berries, and fruits. Meat and poultry made their way to the menu much later.

How can our scientists be so sure about the diet of our ancestors who lived millions of years ago? Here's the logic. In the old, wild days the food was not cooked, so there are clear differences between the teeth of those who ate meat and those who ate berries and nuts. On studying the skull of the Australopithecus Afarensis and Australopithecus Robustus, scientists have found no evidence of meat eating – they found them to have small grinding teeth that are usually present in animals who feed on wild berries and nuts.

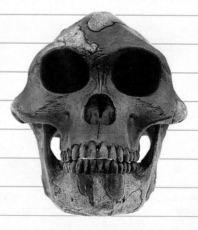

What's more, anthropologists have also studied the stomachs of primates and come up with interesting discoveries. They observed that for millions of years, the only food that went into the stomachs of our ancestors was vegetables. That's why even the stomachs of our ancestors looks different from those of meat-eating mammals back then.

FAST FACT . . .
Once man turned non-vegetarian, his small grinding teeth became long and sharp.

FAST FACT . . .
It is believed that extreme climatic conditions like drought or bitter, freezing cold, which left man with almost no berries, forced our ancestors to turn non-vegetarian.

Of course, it sounds a little bizarre because we've always assumed that primitive man was a non-vegetarian.

31. DEATH RITUALS

If you thought that the rites and rituals accompanying death originated not very long ago, during the Middle Ages at best; think again. The practice of holding funerals started almost about 60,000 years ago during the times of the Neanderthal man. Skulls and other remains of this species have been found along with remnants of flowers.

This finding points towards the fact that Neanderthal man had some customs and rituals for the dead. He mourned; which is why he covered the grave of the dead with flowers. This has lead scientists to ask if this means that these rituals indicate a belief in life after death among these ancient men. Since all

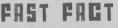
FAST FACT . . .
The oldest known "graves" were found in Shanidar caves in Iraq.

this happened so long ago, and since man himself was not documenting his existence back then, nothing has been confirmed on those fronts yet.

But it does suggest that early man was well aware of the concept of death, which was why he performed these rituals for people who died.

Unlike modern times, the burial tradition during the era of the Neanderthal man didn't involve digging a deep pit. Instead, the body was placed on the ground and covered with mud, stones, plants, and flowers. Sometimes the corpses were even left in the open on a raised platform or amidst the plants.

FAST FACT . . .

According to the Egyptian mummification rules, the wealthier you are, the better is the state of your mummy. That's probably because rich people could afford more elaborate mummification techniques.

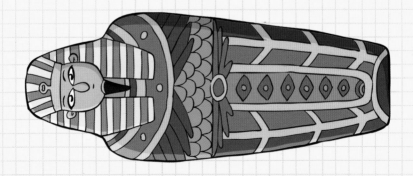

32. NATIVE AMERICANS

We know that ancient humans didn't dig pits for the dead, but instead they covered the deceased's body with mud, stone, plants, and other such things that made the burial place look like a mound. Slowly, as societies evolved, man started adding details to these mounds, which gave rise to the prestigious profession of Mound Builders.

Amongst the first Mound Builders were the Native Americans. Many of these mounds are found in the Mississippi and Ohio valleys. This is what makes archeologists suggest that it could be the Native Americans who specialized in this profession and were the first to start an organized system of burial.

Three different kinds of mounds were built – burial, effigy, and platform mounds. A burial mound is conical in shape and apart from the body of the deceased it contains his/her favorite things, such as jewelry, toys, utensils, etc. An effigy mound is in the shape of an animal or bird, and it represents totems.

FAST FACT . . .
There are 24 burial mounds in the Mound City Group National Monument in Ohio.

Platform mounds are generally places of worship; they are formed on a raised platform and are surrounded by residential areas where priests and other people of importance live.

FAST FACT . . .

An example of the platform mound is the Fort Ancient in Warren County, Ohio.

33. HUMAN EMOTIONS

The fear of death is at the root of every human emotion. That's the basis of Terror Management Theory! This theory has been put forward by American anthropologist Ernest Becker. According to it, all cultures are distractions to keep us from thinking about death.

Almost all of us are afraid to die. Even so, we have a tendency to hang on to things as if they're going to last forever. Maybe our psychology has developed in such a way that it keeps the thoughts of inevitable death at bay. But, according to Becker, it's not just us, it's the effort of the entire humanity to ignore the truth, as if it didn't exist. For those who were still paranoid about the fact, religions and cultures were said to be created as distractions.

FAST FACT . . .

Neophobia is the fear of anything new. If you feel uncomfortable with certain new ideas, you might just have Neophobia!

34. HUNTER-GATHERERS

Societies of hunter-gatherers are still found in parts of Asia, Africa, and South America. There, groups of about 20-50 people move together, hunting and gathering food as they go.

An egalitarian lifestyle is a very peaceful set-up where members of the society decide upon individual autonomy. There is no hierarchy in such a system, and everyone is treated as equal.

The values that are of prime importance in an egalitarian set-up are co-operation, sharing, non-violence, making consensual decisions, and non-directive child-bearing methods.

In this kind of set-up, no one is wealthier than another because everyone shares. Anthropologists are awed by this kind of a peaceful set-up, especially in such primitive tribes. Usually, primitive tribes are viewed as violent or barbaric, but that is clearly not true in the case of hunter-gatherers.

35. HUNTER-GATHERERS

Hunter-gatherers were very particular about their ethos. They actively wanted to follow egalitarian ways, so they kept a strict watch for any slip-ups in attitude. That's because in an egalitarian set-up, attitude could make or break the deal.

When the hunter-gatherers decided that they want a way of life in which all are treated as equals, they decided to follow the concept of reverse dominance. In this kind of a set-up, no man or woman is allowed to throw his or her weight around, and all members of the society must do equal amounts of work and share the produce with everyone. If anyone tried to become the leader, the entire community would team up against that person and he/she was made to understand that such behavior was not acceptable.

These communities had a unique way of keeping their members in line. There was no legal system, jail, or punishment back then.

Nevertheless, the hunter-gatherers came up with an ingenious method to make sure everyone followed the norms of the tribe. The erring member was teased! He was bullied and teased endlessly about his unacceptable behavior, until he understood that such behavior would not be tolerated by the rest.

FAST FACT . . .
If teasing didn't help, the society members would shun the offender. The person was either forced to mend his ways, or move away from the group.

36. HUNTING TRIBES

The earliest societies in the world were the hunting and gathering types, in which Man had just started organizing himself. The primitive way of getting food in those times was to either hunt or pluck berries and nuts from trees.

The hunter-gatherers' communities were nomadic societies who kept moving from one place to another. When they had finished eating all the berries from the neighboring trees and feasted on the animals around, they moved on. The work of such societies was equally divided amongst the members. Whatever surplus food was left was stored. This was the first basic unit of an organized society.

FAST FACT . . .
These basic tribes also had a set of rituals and customs that they strictly followed.

FAST FACT . . .
Sometimes these societies stumbled upon an area with abundant food and would settle down into stable villages.

37. CHILDREN IN TRIBES

We have read with great interest how the hunter-gatherer societies came to be. Apart from their means of livelihood, there's one more interesting thing about this society, and that's their relationship with their children.

Actually, such societies exist even today, people who have researched these tribes report that parents in such societies do not believe in punishing their children. They do not prohibit their children from exploring and experimenting.

The children in these societies were allowed to play from dawn to dusk, which gave them a rather cheerful disposition, and a very positive outlook on life. Even the grown-ups performed their duties in a playful mood! Imagine living in a society where even work was play?

38. PASTORAL SOCIETIES

Humans in pastoral societies settled down in places with large pastures where they could rear cattle. They had their own pet cattle that provided for the food requirements of the society. Pastoral societies are still found in certain remote areas.

When man started moving from one place to another, he came across large green pastures. These were places that didn't receive a great amount of rainfall, and could only sustain grass. Not many shrubs or trees were available for food. Man found that cattle such as cows and sheep loved these places as they had lots of fodder to graze on.

So man started domesticating cattle and developed pastoral societies. These societies sustained themselves by selling the milk and milk products of the cattle to the neighboring societies. Man found this kind of settlement far more comfortable than his previous hunting and gathering kinds.

Thus man began to settle down in one place, as he could stay on these pastures for a long time, until his cattle had exhausted all the grass. Man began to save a lot of energy that he used to spend looking for new places to settle down, and began to develop other professions. Apart from the cattle business, some people from these societies also became traders, fortune tellers, craftsmen, etc.

FAST FACT . . .

Pastoral societies emerged around 12,000 years ago.

39. HORTICULTURAL SOCIETIES

These societies, too, were nomadic in nature because they relied on fruits and vegetables growing in the area for their sustenance. Unlike the gatherer-kinds, horticultural societies were slightly more advanced. They knew how to grow their own food. They grew fruits, vegetables, and plants, and relied on selling fruits for their sustenance.

Horticultural societies settle down at different places and sell their produce to the neighboring areas. Whenever their produce is in surplus, they store it for future use. These societies use various kinds of cultivation techniques

FAST FACT . . .
Horticulture comes from the Latin word hortus, which means "garden."

like slash and burn, shifting agriculture, and swidden cultivation. According to such techniques, the land must be left empty every two years for it to replenish all its lost nutrients. Children played an important role here because they were usually entrusted with the work of weeding.

40. AGRICULTURAL SOCIETIES

When man learnt the technique of agriculture, he developed ways to grow grains like wheat, rice, corn, and barley. This change in society has been termed as an "Agricultural Revolution" by sociologists.

As the technologies and skill of growing crops evolved, man started growing food in surplus. Slowly, huge towns sprang up around the agricultural land. Various professions also began to pop up, because people now had more free time on their hands. The town became abuzz with a lot of people who were farmers, traders, merchants, religious leaders, and teachers. This led to the division of society.

FAST FACT . . .

During the 1800s, new machines like reaping and threshing machines were invented to perform tasks that had previously been done by hand. This advancement marks the beginning of the "Agricultural Revolution."

41. FEUDAL SOCIETIES

These kinds of societies developed between the 9th and the 15th centuries and thrived when agricultural societies began dividing themselves into different strata. Certain people emerged as the affluent class. These were the feudal lords.

Feudal lords were the owners of fertile land. They were the ones who generally employed poor people to work on the land as farmers in return for security and food. Feudal lords usually exploited the poor farmers and made them work as slaves.

In the Middle Ages, the King would give away large chunks of land to nobles and other people of importance. These gifts were known as "fiefs." The people who came to own such lands eventually became the feudal lords while the people, or peasants, who worked on these lands were called "serfs." The serfs were forced to work for the feudal lord in return for security. These serfs, according to the Medieval Law, didn't even "belong to" themselves; they were the property of the feudal lords and worked on the lands like slaves.

It was around the 15th century that this system began to pave way for capitalism, when trade routes opened up and people from different lands started intermingling.

FAST FACT . . .
People did not live very long during the Middle Ages because of the deplorable human conditions prevalent at the time. Most people died before the age of 30.

FAST FACT . . .
90 percent of the people during that time worked as peasants.

42. BARTER SYSTEM

This kind of financial system involves goods being exchanged in place of goods. It does not involve money at all. Understandably, it was the means of trade before money was invented. In fact, almost all ancient civilizations followed it.

The barter system dates back to 6000 B.C. It was first introduced by the Mesopotamian tribe and was later taken up by Phoenicians. The system was developed by the Babylonians who bartered huge amounts of goods across the seas. Various items were worth different amounts. Salt, for example, was a popular item in barter system, which is how the saying "worth your salt" was born. People exchanged many things for salt, because salt was necessarily used by soldiers to preserve food items and so it was of prime importance in every state. At one point, human skulls were used to buy things!

The disadvantage of this barter system was that there was no means of checking if the goods being exchanged were of good quality. The chances of getting duped increased manifold. Yet, the system worked because no money was involved.

FAST FACT . . .
During the Great Depression in the 1930s, money was scarce. During this period, the barter system became popular again.

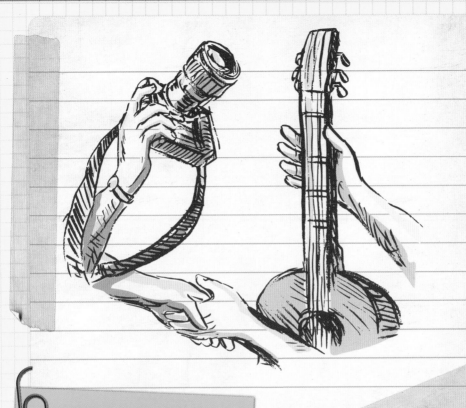

FAST FACT . . .
The Europeans bartered crafts and fur for silk and perfume.

43. INDUSTRIAL SOCIETIES

The invention of the steam engine in the 18th century gave rise to the Industrial Revolution. This revolution brought about a major change in societies. Fuel-driven machines had made their way into the human civilization, and that changed the way the societies worked.

As the production of crops increased, man started needing more help. It was around this time that the Industrial Revolution unfolded. Farming turned mechanized, and the invention of the steam engine meant that goods could now be easily transported to far-off places. It was a great leap.

Gradually, as trends changed, the demand for food increased. To meet the growing demand, the first cottage industries began to be set up. As these industries grew, so did the need for larger industries.

The Industrial Revolution was born in Britain. Before the revolution, everyone's life revolved around farming, and diseases and malnutrition were very common, but industrial societies changed all that. Slowly, people started settling around the industries.

FAST FACT . . .
Large cities had started emerging with a varied class of people, such as bureaucrats and the elite.

Initially, just the people who worked in the industries shifted, but later people who could provide other services, such as astrologers, traders, and craftsmen, also began settling around these industries.

44. POST-INDUSTRIAL SOCIETIES

After the Industrial Revolution came another wave that knocked the hats off societies and ushered in a new era – the post-industrial era. This was facilitated by the invention of computers. The focus was now shifting from physical labor to intellect, and people began to form organizations based on the gray matter between man's ears.

The most exciting thing about this era is that we are right in the middle of it! In this kind of a society, we focus on the know-hows and knowledge of technologies, and importance is given to education and training. As the post-industrial society progresses, sociologists hope that mankind will start focusing on the welfare of the society rather than on social status. This will help decrease social conflict.

The revolution that brought about this change was called the Information Revolution or the "Third Wave." It has made people open up their minds. Sociologists believe that the burst of information has ensured a just society. Democracy usually rules in this type of a setup. Sociologists are also of the opinion that because of the invention of the wireless media, people will now be able to take part in political decision-making.

FAST FACT . . .

Almost 65 percent of the people in Western Countries are employed in the information sector.

PUNIC WARS

DICTATORSHIP

CRUSADES

CIVIL WAR

DEMOCRACY

FRENCH REVOLUTION

CHEROKEE

NIXON

THE STUDY OF POLITICS

TRAIL OF TEARS

NAZI

WORLD WARS

MARCO POLO

SUFFRAGE

VIETNAM WAR

HITLER

45. TYPES OF GOVERNMENTS

There are close to 200 countries in the world, and with so many independent countries, there are bound to be several different types of governments. There are, in totality, seven different types of governments that rule the world.

A government is a political body that looks after the people of the State – the citizens – but how does a government come into power? The different ways in which a government is elected gives rise to seven different types of governments.

Democracy:

A democracy is a government of the people, by the people, and for the people. The people vote for their government and decide who their leader will be.

Dictatorship:

Here, a single person has come to power by force and has gained control. People under this government do not have a say in the election of their leader.

Monarchy:
This is the system of kings and queens. The head of State remains on the throne for his/her entire life. After the death of the head, the first born of the royal family (in many situations, a younger male has precedence over an eldest daughter though) becomes King or Queen.

Theocracy:
Here, the religious body has influence over all of the State and takes control of it.

Totalitarian:
This governance is where a group of people take control. It's just like dictatorship where an individual has been replaced by a group.

Republics:
This system is similar to a democracy, with the President as the head, while the government office is voted by people.

Anarchy:
A country in a state of political unrest, where a stable government is absent, is called an anarchy.

46. CRUSADES

Jerusalem is a place of great religious importance to Christians, Muslims, and Jews. It was so important that the famous Crusades began when people were barred from making their pilgrimage to this sacred land.

FAST FACT . . .

The first Crusade was called for in 1095.

Jerusalem was a holy land for Christians because it was where Jesus was crucified. For the Muslims, this marked the place where Muhammad had ascended to heaven. For the Jews, it was the site of an ancient temple built by Solomon.

Making a pilgrimage to this land was of utmost importance to all

FAST FACT . . .

A Crusader wore a Red Cross made out of a fabric that was stitched to his shirt or armor.

the three religions. But in 600 CE, the Arabs took control over Jerusalem. The Arabs allowed the Christian and the Jews to stay there only if they paid their taxes on time.

The situation really started getting alarming when a small group of Arabs came to power and they denied access to the Christians and Jews. That's when the Pope decided to call for a crusade – a volunteer army.

Followers of both the religions were called upon by their religious leaders to fight against this injustice. Many people dove into this conflict to earn the right to make a pilgrimage to the sacred land.

47. PUNIC WARS

In 256 B.C., the Roman Empire was at its strongest. It had conquered almost the entire Italian peninsula but there was just one land that it couldn't win – Carthage. The Punic Wars are wars fought between Rome and Carthage.

FAST FACT . . .

General Hannibal of Carthage attacked Rome in 221 B.C. and took the city by surprise.

The colonies of Carthage were all round the Mediterranean and the Romans were worried that Carthage would take over the Straight of Messina. So, the Romans destroyed the Carthaginian colonies. That triggered the Punic Wars.

The Carthaginians were quite adept at sea warfare. The Romans, however, took some time to build their fleet. Finally, towards the end of the war, the Romans defeated the Carthaginians and gained control over some of its parts.

48. FRENCH REVOLUTION

The period of the French revolution resulted in a makeover of the French political system. It took place during the time of Napoleon Bonaparte and marked the end of monarchy and feudal systems in France.

not have any bread, she said "Then let them have cake." The monarchy's detachment from their subjects took them to the guillotine within a few years of the famous Storming of the Bastille. After the revolution, unjust institutions like that of feudal lords and absolute monarchy were ousted in favor of a Republic.

The French Revolution went on almost for a decade, beginning in 1789 and ending in the late 1790s. Legend says that the revolt was triggered by Queen Mary Antoinette's response to the public's grievances. It is said that when she heard that the people were hungry and did

FAST FACT . . .
The first public zoo in France was created during the French Revolution.

49. MARCO POLO

Marco Polo is known for his travelogue, "The Travels of Marco Polo." Did you know that his claim to fame was actually written when he was in prison? How could someone so famous spend any time behind bars? What was he imprisoned for? And how did he get out? Read on to find out!

he actually led a small army to war. It's true! It happened three years after Marco Polo returned from his famous journey, when there was a war going on between Venice and Genoa, a rival Italian state. Marco Polo led a small band into Genoa to fight the war.

It was during this that he was arrested. While in prison, he

We're all well aware of Marco Polo's love for travel and adventure, but we're not all that well-versed with the fact that

FAST FACT . . .
"The Travels of Marco Polo" is otherwise known as "The Million."

shared space with Rustichello of Pisa, who was known for his romantic verses. Marco Polo began to narrate the stories of his travels, and Rustichello noted all of them down. In a way, Rustichello was a ghost-writer for "The Travels of Marco Polo."

By 1299, when both friends were out of prison, the book was complete. So, Marco Polo is a household name today only because of his sojourn in prison. Had his adventures not been immortalized there, he would have been yet another forgotten traveler, and not the famous adventurer he is today.

FAST FACT . . .
Revealing about his travels on his death bed, Marco Polo said, "I have not told half of what I saw."

FAST FACT . . .
Marco Polo's adventures were said to have inspired Christopher Columbus.

50. GREAT WALL OF CHINA

Emperor Qin Shin Huang was the first to think of building such a great structure that would run for thousands of miles. He did so in order to keep out the barbaric nomadic tribes.

FAST FACT . . .
The Great Wall of China is the longest man-made structure on Earth.

The Great Wall of China is not really one long wall; it has many walls and fortifications running along with it. Though it was Emperor Qin Shin Huang (259–210 B.C.) who thought of constructing it, it was actually built over a span of 300 years by many different dynasties!

Although built between the 14th and 17th century to keep invaders out, the wall did not really serve to deter invaders and only proved to be a psychological barrier between China and the rest of the world.

FAST FACT . . .
The Great Wall of China is one of the Seven Wonders of the World.

FAST FACT . . .

The Great Wall of China is disconnected at some places, and was built by different dynasties.

FAST FACT . . .

Many people died building the Great Wall of China, which is why it is also termed as the longest cemetery on Earth.

51. GUERILLA WARFARE

As countries waged wars against each other, various conflict techniques were developed. One of these techniques was called "guerilla warfare." This kind of war is usually fought when one party is too weak and small and the enemy is big.

The smaller party breaks all the rules of war and resorts to deception and ambush. It is best suited for uneven terrain, which offers many hiding places. Major Robert Rogers of Connecticut is known to have invented this technique during the French and Indian Wars with America between 1754 and 1763. In this sort of warfare, those engaging in guerilla warfare hide and then ambush the opponent when they least expect it.

The orthodox or traditional military usually gets frustrated by the methods of the guerillas, who strike when least expected. This is why guerillas have been termed as rebels, irregulars, barbarians, terrorists, outlaws, brigades, and other derogatory terms.

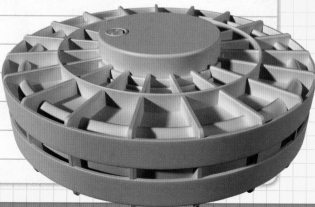

This kind of warfare usually takes place when the guerillas are supported by a large mass of people. They turn to guerilla warfare due to a shortage of ammunitions. Their greatest advantage is the surprise with which they take their enemy, which makes up for other weaknesses they may have.

FAST FACT . . .

In 1765, an academy called Rogers's Royal American Rangers trained people in guerilla warfare.

52. THE TRAIL OF TEARS

This is the story of a very sad journey in history. This journey began from Cherokee in Georgia and ended in Oklahoma. It took place because the Cherokee people were forced by American troops to move out of their homeland.

It all began in 1835 when the Supreme Court granted permission to the Cherokee people to stay in a part of Georgia. After years of living there, when the Cherokee people were happily settled, fate took a turn for worse.

A small group of people amongst the Cherokees turned greedy and signed a treaty that allowed the USA to displace them from their residential land. According to the treaty, the Cherokee people were to settle in the "Indian territory" of Oklahoma. The Cherokee population was devastated when they learnt that they would have to leave their homes and migrate to somewhere new.

FAST FACT . . .
The Cherokees call this journey "Nunahi-Duna-Dlo-Hilu-I." It means the "Trail where they cried."

The Cherokee people showed resistance, but all in vain. The American troops moved in and emptied the land.

The journey from Georgia to Oklahoma was a difficult one and filled with sadness. Many of the Cherokee people died and many were injured, and many tears were shed during this journey, giving it the name, "The Trail of Tears."

FAST FACT . . .
The act by which Cherokees were removed was called the Removal Act of 1830.

53. WOMEN'S SUFFRAGE

History bears witness to the struggle that women endured to achieve equality with men in some areas of law. One of the most famous women's right movements was the Women's Suffrage Movement. Thanks to this initiative, men and women now have a greater sense of equality in society.

smart enough for selecting the leaders of the country. Finally, a bunch of women put their foot down and said, "Enough!"

The first step towards the Women's Suffrage Movement was taken by Elizabeth Cady Stanton, Lucretia Mott, Lucy Stone, and Susan B. Anthony in 1848. Before this movement, women weren't allowed to vote. The reason behind this was that women weren't considered

The initiation of the movement took place in 1848 in Seneca Falls, New York. The group of ladies, including Elizabeth Cady Stanton, Lucretia Mott, Lucy Stone, and Susan B. Anthony, met up at the national convention and put their views across. This resulted in an "improved" Declaration of Independence.

But it took another 70 years for this first step to finally transform into the "right to vote for women." On August 26, 1920, in the 19th Amendment, women were finally acknowledged and given the status of "equality."

FAST FACT . . .

Elizabeth Cady Stanton allowed Susan B. Anthony to babysit her seven children as she wrote the speeches for the movement.

54. BLACK CODES

Once the Civil War ended in 1865, a period of reconstruction began in the USA. During this, the African-Americans began to assert their freedom and stand up against injustice to their kind. To weaken this, the "black code" was issued.

The "black codes" were passed in Mississippi and South Carolina in late 1865. According to these, African-Americans needed to sign a yearly agreement with their employer which stated that they would not leave their job until the contract was terminated. If they did, they would have to return the wages that had been paid till then. Another rule in the "black code" was that if they held any job other than that of the farmer or the servant, they would have to pay taxes ranging from $10 – $100.

55. FREEDOM SUMMER

There was a lot of friction in America with regard to the right to vote. We are already aware of the Suffrage Movement that women had to go through to gain this right. A similar movement was initiated for African-Americans, called the "Freedom Summer."

This drive comprised of 1,000 out-of-state white population who supported the African American Mississippians. They faced huge resistance from the Ku Klux Klan, the police, and even the State and local authorities.

Freedom Summer was launched in 1964 by the Congress of Racial Equality (CORE) and the Student Non-Violent Coordinating Committee (SNCC) as a voter registration drive to ensure that all people of Mississippi voted, irrespective of their skin color.

FAST FACT . . .

The African Americans couldn't testify against the whites during a trial because of the "Black Code."

56. CIVIL WAR

If the image of the civil war in your head contains only metal bombers and clunky fire machinery, then you're mistaken. That's because hot air balloons – yes, the ones that leisurely float in the sky – were also used during the war.

Both sides – the Union and the Confederate – used hot air balloons to spy on each other during the civil war. The Americans even had an official organization called the "Balloon Corps," sanctioned by none other than Abraham Lincoln, which took care of such expeditions.

Balloon Corps was run under the guidance of a Chief Aeronaut, Thaddeus Lowe. It was he who decided when and how many balloons would go up into the air. The balloons could travel all the way up to 5,000 feet in the air.

Why were these balloons sent up? It was to allow an aerial view for the generals. Floating above in the sky gave the Americans an aerial view of what was going on in the war which helped

FAST FACT . . .
The largest hot air balloon is called Energizer Bunny Hot Hare Balloon. It is 166 feet tall.

them strategize and take stock of the situation. That's what gave the Americans an edge in the war.

FAST FACT . . .
The longest balloon flight was from Japan to North Canada on January 15, 1991, in a balloon called "Virgin Pacific Flyer."

FAST FACT . . .
John Wise, a professional aeronaut, received the first order to build a balloon for the Union army. Unfortunately, this balloon escaped its tethers and was shot down to prevent it from falling into Confederate hands.

57. WORLD WAR I

World War I took place between the Allies and the Central Powers and went on for four years, from 1914 to 1918. Do you know what actually triggered this great, big, bloody war?

It's public knowledge that there were many issues between the Allies and the Central Power. The Allies included Russia, France, the British Empire, Italy, USA, Japan, Romania, Serbia, Belgium, Greece, Portugal, and Montenegro. The Central Powers included Germany, Austria-Hungary, Turkey, and Bulgaria.

There was a tug-of-war of sorts between these two groups over territories and empires. What actually triggered the start of the war on June 28, 1914, was the murder of Archduke Franz

FAST FACT . . .

Over 8 million troops died and 21 million were wounded in World War I.

Ferdinand of Austria and his pregnant wife. The Archduke was the nephew of the reigning Emperor of Austria and Hungary, and the assassination was planned by a Serbian group. These assassinations infuriated the Central Powers and the cascading events led to one of the biggest wars the world has ever seen.

The culmination of all the unrest preceding this incident and the incident itself triggered World War I. The war was so huge that it was even called "The War to End All Wars," "The Wars of The Nations," and "The Great War."

Ironically though, this bloody war did not end all wars, because World War II followed shortly after.

FAST FACT . . .

The chemical weapon "mustard gas" was first used in World War I.

58. PEARL HARBOR

The story of Pearl Harbor began when Japan took control over a chunk of land that lay between China and Russia – Manchuria. After that, Japan began eyeing other regions of the southeast and started moving towards China. This is what finally led to the famous Pearl Harbor Attack.

Japan had gained control over Manchuria in 1931. Angered by this, the USA decided to cut the ties between them.

The USA stopped supplying oil to Japan, but Japan had thought it through and already made arrangements to import oil from Asian countries instead. However, Japan did not foresee that the US naval troops peppered all over the sea would make this an extremely difficult task. Frustrated by these unforeseen complications, Japan decided to attack one of the prime points of the US navy – Pearl Harbor.

Japan secretly planned the whole attack and, on December 7, 1941, Pearl Harbor was attacked. In the strike, 21 ships of the US Navy fleet were destroyed and 2,400 people were killed.

FAST FACT . . .
The day after the attack on Pearl Harbor is known as the Day of the Infamy Speech, because of the speech that President Roosevelt gave on that day.

This unforeseen and uncalled-for attack forced the USA to abandon its position of neutrality and enter the war. USA declared war on Japan and entered World War II. Japan sided with Germany but was eventually defeated by the USA after the Hiroshima and Nagasaki bombings.

FAST FACT . . .
Pearl Harbor is visited by 1.5 million people every year.

59. HIROSHIMA AND NAGASAKI

The bombing of Hiroshima and Nagasaki is considered to be one of the most horrific bombings in history. The effects of the tragedy are clearly visible even today.
The radioactive material used in the bombs has spread throughout the atmosphere, water, and vegetation. Even today children are born with genetic defects caused due to that radiation.

During World War II, in 1945, Japan was asked to surrender to the Allied powers. Japan refused. The country was then warned that if it refused to surrender, it would face "prompt and utter destruction."

The first bomb, which was called the "Little Boy," was dropped on Hiroshima on the morning of August 6, 1945. It destroyed an area of five square miles. The second bomb was called the "Fat Man" and was dropped on Nagasaki three days later on August 9, 1945. Even though this was stronger than the first one, it destroyed only 2.6 square miles of the area, because of the topography of Nagasaki. The two cities were almost wiped out by the impact of the two nuclear bombs.

FAST FACT . . .
August 15 is celebrated as Victory in Japan or V-J Day.

After these two devastating attacks, on the noon of August 15, 1945, Emperor Hirohito surrendered on the radio.

FAST FACT . . .

The surrender agreement was signed in the sky in an airplane called "Missouri."

60. ADOLF HITLER

We all know about the atrocities that were committed by Adolf Hitler — merely mentioning the concentration camps is enough to send shivers down many spines. Then again, many are in awe of Hitler's method of administration and control. Whatever the case, we know scant little about the other facets of his personality.

Adolf Hitler was born in Austria on April 20, 1889. "Adi," as he was known in his youth, had four siblings — Gustav, Ida, Otto, and Edmund — who passed away when he was just a child. It wasn't Hitler's childhood dream to become a dictator; in fact, Hitler wanted to become an

FAST FACT . . .

Hitler was arrested in 1923 when he tried to take over the German government. While he was in prison, he wrote his autobiography, "Mein Kampf" (My Struggle).

FAST FACT . . .
During World War I, Hitler was grievously injured twice – once by a splintered grenade and the second time by a gas attack, when he temporarily went blind.

artist – he even applied twice to the Vienna Academy of Arts. However, life had other plans in store for him.

After he was orphaned, Hitler sold postcards on the streets of Vienna. After that, he joined the German Army. He survived World War I and quickly rose up the ranks. He was even awarded two Iron Crosses for his bravery. The rest of his life story is known to most. We also know that he committed suicide to end his life, but most don't know that it was the day after he got married to his girlfriend, Eva Baum, on April 29, 1930.

61. HOLOCAUST

The word "Holocaust" originates from the Greek word for sacrificial burning at the altar. But the word's connotations changed at the Nazi camps, where many people were tortured to death. These death camps were the brainchild of Adolf Hitler during World War II.

were taken to concentration camps built by the Nazis. Hordes of people were packed into freight trains and taken to such extermination camps. Many people died during the journey itself, but those who survived only had to face systematic killing in the gas chambers on arrival. Those who avoided the gas chambers

According to Hitler, the Jews brought impurities into the German race and so should be eradicated. He also blamed them for Germany's loss in World War I. Laws were passed against the Jews, such as the Nuremberg Laws in 1935, that advocated the killing of Jews. These legislations began before the outbreak of World War II, and the Jews and certain others

FAST FACT . . .

The term "Nazi" is an acronym for "Nationalsozialistishe Deutsche Arbeiterpartei" which translates to "National Socialist German Worker's Party."

FAST FACT . . .
Approximately six million Jewish people were killed during the Holocaust.

were made to work as slaves until they died of exhaustion.

While it's well-known that the movement was primarily against the Jews, there were certain other people who were targeted. Gypsies and homosexuals, among many others, were also persecuted during this regime, because they were also considered impure by the Nazis.

FAST FACT . . .
Around 1.1 million of the people murdered during the Holocaust were children.

62. THE NAZI PARTY

The Nazi Party was the better-known name for the National Socialist German Workers' Party, which was led by Adolf Hitler. It ruled Germany from 1933 to 1945 and promoted anti-Semitism.

The Nazi Party was founded in 1919, due to the unhappiness that rose from the terms of the Treaty of Versailles. Hitler became the leader in 1921 and, when the Nazis came to power in 1933, he assumed a dictatorship in Germany.

The Nazi Party went out of power only once Germany was defeated in World War II.

Though most of its top officials were convicted of the murder of 6 million European Jews, a few still remain at large.

FAST FACT . . .
Topics of education under the Nazi regime included racial biology, population policy, culture, geography, and physical fitness.

63. D-DAY

This historic event took place during World War II and the story of D-Day is full of surprises. On June 6, 1944, the Allied forces launched an attack on the Germans on the coast of Normandy, in France.

What makes this such an important day in history is the fact that the Germans were caught unaware and it changed the course of events in World War II. While the Germans had an idea that the Allied forces were preparing for an invasion, they had no clue that 150,000 soldiers would attack the coast of Normandy on June 6, 1944. This came as a shock, and led to the Germans losing the war.

FAST FACT . . .

The invasion was due to take place on June 5, but bad weather delayed the attack.

FAST FACT . . .

Around two years were spent planning the medical treatment of the wounded. At the onset of the invasion, 30,000 stretchers and 60,000 blankets were made ready.

64. COLD WAR

The Cold War went on for around 50 years – from 1945 to 1991. It was a tension that was built between the democracies and the communists of the world, which set the West, led by the USA, against Eastern Europe, led by the Soviet Union.

This war was called the "Cold War" because there was no direct fight between the USA and Soviet Union. Instead they fought proxy wars. This means that they supported warring countries. Examples of proxy wars include the Vietnam War and the Korean War.

But while proxy wars are a way of showing animosity, the two super powers even resorted to showing off their weapons.

The two superpowers decided to give a cold shoulder to each other after World War II came to an end in 1945, when the

FAST FACT . . .
The two superpowers took part in an Arms Race to show off their nuclear bombs.

Allies stopped supporting the Soviet Union. This action led to the disintegration of the Soviet Union and the Cold War finally came to an end in 1991.

The two superpowers also tried to show their muscle by advancing their space technology, which is why the period of the Cold War was one of great scientific advancement too.

65. PRESIDENT NIXON

Richard Nixon lost the trust of his people after the Watergate scandal was exposed. But why was it such a big deal? And why wasn't Nixon ever prosecuted? There are certain answers we might never know.

It all began early one morning on June 17, 1972. A group of five men who worked for the CIA (Central Intelligence Agency) were caught at 2.30 a.m. in the office of the Democratic National Committee at Watergate. On investigation, it was revealed that the intruders were, in some way, connected to Nixon's re-election campaign.

FAST FACT . . .

Richard Nixon even tried to stop the Federal Bureau of Investigation (FBI) from getting to the bottom of the case.

However, there was no convincing evidence of this. It wasn't even clear whether Nixon knew about this operation.

GERALD FORD 1974-1977

FAST FACT . . .

The next President, Gerald Ford, pardoned Nixon, which is why Richard Nixon was never prosecuted for the Watergate Scandal.

It might have still ended well for Nixon, except that he started behaving suspiciously. People noticed that Nixon was trying his best to hush the case and even began firing staff that refused to co-operate with him. He also destroyed a recording that could have been used as evidence.

People started to notice his behavior and began to ask questions. Finally, due to public pressure, Nixon resigned.

66. THE VIETNAM WAR

The Vietnam War was one of the longest wars in history. It was a battle between the Communists and the Republics. Finally, at the end of those long years, the communists, led by Ho Chi Minh, emerged victorious.

FAST FACT . . .
Around two-thirds of the American troops serving in the Vietnam War were volunteers.

The two forces that were pitted against each other in the Vietnam War were the Communist North Vietnamese forces and the anti-Communist coalition forces. The Communist North Vietnamese forces were led by Ho Chi Minh, and were supported by Viet Cong in South Vietnam, the People's Republic of China, and the Soviet Union. The anti-Communist coalition forces, on the other hand, were made up of the Republic of Vietnam from South Vietnam, the USA, South Korea, Australia, New Zealand, Thailand, and Laos. The Vietnam War was also a

part of the Cold War, where the USA and the Soviet Union were pitted against each other.

After 19½ years, in March 1973, the USA and other foreign countries that were supporting the anti-Communist coalition withdrew their support. And on April 30, 1975, Saigon, the South Vietnamese capital, fell to the Communists, bringing an end to the Vietnam War.

FAST FACT . . .
The Vietnam War is the longest war in the history of the USA.

67. THE BYZANTINE EMPIRE

The Byzantine Empire was formed in 330 A.D. when the Roman Empire was split into the Eastern and Western Empires. The Eastern part formed the Byzantine Empire. While the Western Empire collapsed in 476 CE, the Byzantine Empire continued for another 1000 years.

north east. He finally reached the Greek city of Chalcedon and thought that its founders must have been blind, because they had chosen to ignore the obviously superior site only half a mile away and settle there.

The story of the origin of the name "Byzantium" is an interesting one. In 660 B.C., Byas, a Greek citizen, wished to form a new colony, since the mainland of Greece was too populated. He consulted an oracle, which simply whispered, "opposite the blind."

Though he didn't understand the message, he simply sailed

So, he founded his settlement opposite Chalcedon and named it Byzantium after himself.

FAST FACT . . .
The city of Constantinople was attacked during the Fourth Crusade by Crusaders.

68. CU CHI TUNNELS

Cu Chi Tunnels were used as guerilla warfare techniques by the Viet Cong (VC) to fight against Americans and South Vietnamese. These tunnels were 10,000 miles long.

FAST FACT . . .

These tunnels are located in the Vietnam War Memorial Park and are a great tourist attraction today.

The Cu Chi tunnels are a network of tunnels under the Cu Chi district. It was built by the Viet Cong so they could surprise or shock their enemies by popping up and disappearing from various places with the help of these tunnels as a form of guerilla warfare.

The USA and South Vietnamese soldiers who were trained to use these tunnels were known as "tunnel rats." Their job was to find a way through the extensive network and detect all hidden booby traps.

ATTENTION

PAVLOV

MULTI-TASKING

DAY-DREAMING

ZONING OUT

SALIVATION

APRIL FOOL'S DAY

PLACEBO

SARCASM

PSYCHOLOGY

DOGS

CLASSICAL CONDITIONING

69. SARCASM

Sarcasm is something most of us are fine with, until it is directed towards us. But, as they say, there's always a silver lining. Turns out, being sarcastic can actually make you smarter! How? Read on!

A study was conducted in 2011 on this topic. It turns out that we use relatively fewer brain cells to decipher straightforward remarks as compared to sarcastic remarks. Straightforward comments require basic comprehension, whereas sarcastic comments require the brain to function at several different levels, thereby making the brain work harder.

So to comprehend a sarcastic remark, the brain has to exercise more of its gray cells, which can make your brain more active and therefore more smart!

"I forgot to put a smiley face on my sarcastic email to you."

FAST FACT . . .
The study also revealed that the use of sarcasm soared during chat sessions.

70. APRIL FOOL'S DAY

April 1 is a day on which everyone indulges their juvenile tendencies and plays tricks on one another. It's the official prank day. Have you ever wondered how an entire day came to be dedicated just to pranks and pranksters?

In 1582, when France adopted the Georgian calendar, the New Year shifted from April 1 to January 1. A few people were unaware of this change and continued to wish each other a happy new year on April 1. Those who were in fact aware of the change had a hearty laugh, and so the tradition continues.

FAST FACT . . .

The Scottish love this day so much that they celebrate April Fool's Day for two days!

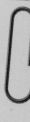

FAST FACT . . .

In Belgium, on April Fool's Day, children lock their parents out and open the door only if they are promised sweets.

APRIL FOOL's DAY

2011
APRIL

1

71. SALIVATING DOGS

This study was one of the landmark studies in the history of psychology. It is an extremely famous study in which Ivan Pavlov trained dogs to salivate on hearing a bell. Pavlov stumbled upon this discovery quite by accident. He wasn't even a psychologist – he was a physiologist.

Pavlov was actually studying the salivation response of dogs when they were eating. Suddenly, Pavlov noticed that dogs began salivating even when they weren't eating. Every time he walked into the room (with or without food) his dogs' mouths began watering.

Apart from throwing his experiment completely off track, this was also rather messy, considering the number of times Pavlov had to walk into a room filled with drooling dogs. Imagine the amount of saliva he'd have to clean up all the time!

Pavlov realized that his dogs had learned to salivate just by looking at him.

What was even more astonishing is that salivation itself is an involuntary response. You can't control when you salivate. Could he actually be able to train his dogs to salivate on demand?

He then realized that it wasn't just him that made the dogs' mouth water, but anything that the dogs associated with their food, such as the lab assistants, or even the sound of the bell that was rung before the dogs were given their food. The sound was enough to trigger a pool of drool.

FAST FACT . . .
There was a series of experiments conducted by American Psychologist John Watson, called the "Little Albert Experiments" in which he used a loud gong and a white mouse to scare a child named Albert. Soon the child was scared of not just the mouse, but also other white, fluffy objects like rabbits. Of course, this is unethical and would not be allowed today.

This process of training an involuntary response is called classical conditioning and it has been applied extensively in contemporary psychology.

FAST FACT . . .
Classical conditioning can even be used to induce the fear of an object in a person.

72. THE PLACEBO EFFECT

We often underestimate the role our mind plays on our physical well-being. Sometimes, all it takes is a doctor to tell us "You'll be fine." That can actually make us start feeling better already. This effect is what psychologists call "the Placebo Effect."

A placebo is a sugar pill, with no actual medicinal properties. Many studies have been carried out on this subject, where patients complaining of physical symptoms like back aches or headaches were given placebos. However, they were not told that it's just a sugar pill. Instead, they were told that

it's a new, improved drug that is guaranteed to make them feel better.

Surprisingly, a lot of the people taking the sugar pill actually reported feeling better, and often their symptoms also disappeared. Of course, they never really found out that they were simply popping sugar pills.

FAST FACT . . .
Sometimes, the Placebo effect works even when you know you are being given a placebo! It seems that just the act of taking a pill may be curative.

This is why, when new drugs are developed, they are checked for this effect to confirm that they are actually effective.

FAST FACT . . .
The Placebo effect takes place in animals like dogs too!

FAST FACT . . .
This effect seems to be more prominent in the USA than other parts of the world. Perhaps this has something to do with the large number of medication advertisements that we are exposed to.

73. ZONING OUT

Have you noticed how every morning, the entire routine of brushing your teeth, packing your bags, and eating your breakfast seems almost automatic? You probably don't even remember what you were thinking about while you performed all these tasks!

Our mind works in bizarre ways. Over the years, evolution has ensured that we adapt to changes so that our mind can make the most of what is available. One such evolutionary technique is what we commonly call "zoning out."

While performing habitual tasks that don't really require your full attention and focus, usually tasks that you have been performing for years and have perfected, your mind tends to wander. It is actually beneficial to daydream, or zone out. Times like these are often those of heightened creativity. It is usually when you are dreaming that great ideas hit you!

Also, this process is almost involuntary. You won't be able to stop your mind from wandering even if you wanted to.

complete attention.

You will notice that when people first learn how to drive, they cannot hold a conversation simultaneously. However, driving is almost second nature to drivers who are habituated to it.

FAST FACT . . .
Sometimes, you can perform two or more automatic tasks at the same time, because neither requires much mental energy. People often call this multi-tasking.

FAST FACT . . .
You can zone out about five times during a reading session of 45 minutes.

So perhaps there is some truth to the saying "Practice makes perfect" after all. It seems as though you can perfect almost any task with enough practice!

On the other hand, it is very difficult to day dream when you are performing tasks that you are unfamiliar with and require your

SLAVERY

LABOR DAY

HALLOWEEN

SANTA CLAUS

FUNERAL CUSTOMS

SKY BURIAL

PLAGUE

MUMMIFIED MONKS

SATURNALIA

SOCIOLOGY

DUELS

FOOT BINDING

TEA CEREMONY

74. DUELS

The tradition of duels began in ancient Europe, when there were no courtrooms, lawyers, or law. The rightfulness of one's action was judged by duels back then.

Since ancient times, man has used his strength to flaunt supremacy. Right from the Stone Age, when he hunted for survival, up to the medieval times, when he lived in castles, it is almost as though it is deeply ingrained in his DNA that in order to emerge victorious it is necessary to win a fight.

In the Middle Ages, dueling wasn't just a matter of justice, it became a sport. Knights wanted to show off their strength by holding tournaments amongst themselves. In America, duels popped up along with the first settlers in the 1600s. However, this sport was more prominent in South America than in North America.

Duels hold such a prominent place in human history that such matches were attended by hundreds of people, all wanting to find out who emerged victorious and who got justice. In fact, till date, we witness

FAST FACT . . .
It was in 1621 at Plymouth Rock that the first duel in America took place.

duels – sports like boxing – and enjoy them to the fullest. Who knew that boxing is just a more sophisticated form of dueling?

FAST FACT . . .

Records suggest that around 4,000 nobles lost their lives in duels during the reign of Louis XIV.

75. TEA CEREMONY

The tea ceremony originated as a medicinal ritual. Slowly, as years went by, people started adding their own style and variation to it until it became the great, big, famous "tea ceremony."

Until the ninth century, drinking tea was considered to be purely medicinal. But then, in the 12th century, the Chinese were introduced to "matcha"– a kind of powdered green tea. Slowly, people started devising ways of preparing and drinking matcha and the whole practice of tea-drinking transformed from medicinal to ritual.

In the 13th century, the Samurai Warriors of Japan were introduced to tea-drinking, and they took it along with them to their country. Soon, everyone in Japan got busy drinking tea.

The Japanese tea-drinking wizard, Sen no Rikyu, believed that tea-drinking ceremonies are nothing less than a

sacred ritual. That's because he thought you might meet the people at the ceremony only once. This once-in-a-lifetime meeting should be treated with sincerity and sacredness. That's how the medicinal tea drinking became the large tea ceremony that it is today.

FAST FACT . . .

In a traditional tea ceremony, after sipping the tea, you are supposed to wipe the rim and then set the cup down.

FAST FACT . . .

An elaborate tea ceremony could last for as long as four hours.

76. CHINESE BEAUTY

People have been known to go to strange lengths to ensure beauty, and the Chinese were no less fastidious. To ensure that their ladies had the smallest possible feet, in the seventh century, Chinese families resorted to tying their daughter's feet once she turned six. It was a painful tradition that often caused deformities.

Foot binding is one of the most bizarre and painful traditions in the world. It has been prevalent in China for 2,000 years. Girls were expected to go through this in order to beautify their feet. Of course, by today's standards, deformed feet are by no means beautiful, but certain beliefs are hard to overcome. Who knows, perhaps sometime in the future, a slim body may no longer be considered beautiful?

FAST FACT . . .
Chinese considered tiny feet to be lotus feet.

This ritual usually took place when the girl was around six years old. The girl's feet were soaked in a mixture of herbs and animal blood. Then, after cutting her toenails, her feet were massaged and wrapped tightly in long silk bandages, thereby stunting the foot's growth.

There were special shoes called "foot-binding shoes" or "lotus slippers." These shoes were very small, barely seven and a half centimeters long, because that was considered the ideal length of a woman's foot. Though the shoes were often brightly colored and featured vibrant patterns, every step that the woman took was excruciatingly painful for her.

FAST FACT . . .

The deformities caused by foot-binding prevented women from being independent. They always needed help to move about.

77. MUMMIFIED MONKS

Japanese monks believed that the ritual of mummification would lead to enlightenment. The entire process took about three years and during this time, the monks took care of what they ate so that the process would go smoothly.

Such Buddhist monks who believed and practiced self-mummification were called "Sokushinbutsu." They lived in the northern part of Japan around the Yamagata prefecture. According to this practice, once a monk decided to undergo self-mummification, he took strict care of his diet. For three years, he ate only nuts and seeds and underwent heavy physical activity.

This caused the monk to lose lots of weight, and his body had almost zero fat by the end of the three years.

After three years, the monk began to drink a poisonous tea made from the sap of the Urushi tree. As a result, the monk lost water through diarrhea and vomiting. Almost all the body fluid was lost.

In the final stage the monk locked himself in a stone coffin that was the size of his body. He would breathe through a narrow pipe that was provided and kept ringing a bell. The bell indicated that the monk was alive inside the coffin. Once the bell stopped ringing, the pipe was removed, and the coffin sealed.

FAST FACT . . .
Monks created the first clock in medieval England.

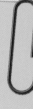

FAST FACT . . .
Monks wear normal footwear. Monks wearing only sandals is a myth.

FAST FACT . . .
The right way to address a monk is to say "Dom."

78. SATURNALIA

If you thought that betting on horses is a new phenomenon, you are quite mistaken. Gambling has been a favorite pastime since ancient times. Of course, the rules and kinds of games that were played differ from the ones we know and play now. Nevertheless, our forefathers most definitely were betting away to glory!

This nugget of history belongs to the time when the Roman Empire was governed by the Emperor Augustus, back in 63 –14 B.C. Just like modern times, gambling was rampant in society, but was not openly allowed. The Emperor had made it illegal. However, there was one loophole in the law.

FAST FACT . . .
Emperor Claudius was fond of the dice games in gambling.

During the festival of Saturnalia, which revolved around the planet Saturn, the Romans were allowed to gamble openly. The elite and the slaves even swapped places during this festival. While the slaves gambled, the elite served them. Talk about role reversal! However, gambling was allowed only during these select days.

FAST FACT . . .
Poker chips were a part of gambling even then.

If you were caught gambling on any other day of the year, you were either fined or punished.

79. THE BLACK DEATH

This horrifying plague landed at the Sicilian Port in Messina, Europe, on 12 Genoese trading ships in 1346. When the Europeans, in their excitement to greet the traders, boarded the ship, they saw that most of the people onboard were dead.

The traders on these ships had fallen prey to the dreadful plague. Even the few that were alive had very high fever and were in a lot of pain. The Sicilian authorities were horrified at the sight. They tried to send the ships back, but it was too late. The plague started spreading on the coast and killed 20 million people in its wake. This epidemic affected every aspect of life in all the towns around the ports. Fields were left unploughed and cattle would roam about untended. This affected the food supply tremendously and the economy came to a standstill.

It was later revealed that the disease spread because of fleas, and it spread quickly due to the rats scurrying in filthy streets. There was almost no country that was left untouched by this deadly disease.

FAST FACT . . .
The Black Death is estimated to have killed 30-60 percent of Europe's population.

FAST FACT . . .
It was later discovered by scientists that the Black Death was caused by a bacillus called "Yersinapestis."

80. MARRIAGE

When man started living in an organized society, there was a need to set some units of family, of how children will be born and who they will belong to. All this led to the idea of marriage – that a man and woman should stay with each other and form a family.

The customs of marriage, and rules about who could marry whom, differed greatly from one civilization to another. For example, it was perfectly fine for first cousins or even brothers and sisters to get married in ancient Egypt. In fact, that's how it usually happened. Queen Cleopatra got married to her brother Ptolemy XIII.

Marriage in those times was based upon political reasoning.

"Love" wasn't one of the prime reason people got married in olden days. Financial security and stability, and alliances between families played a more

FAST FACT . . .
Ancient Romans believed that the circle of the engagement ring denoted eternity.

important role in deciding who would marry whom.

The rituals, ceremonies, and even the reasons for marriage differed from one part of the world to the other. There was only one common thread that ran through all the marriages – the engagement ring.

Everywhere around the world, couples exchanged engagement rings. While in some cases the ring popped up during the proposal, in other cases it was a part of the marriage ceremony.

FAST FACT . . .

There was no concept of romance in or before a marriage in medieval times.

81. TIDONG TRADITIONS

The Tidong people are a minority that started living in Malaysia and are now found in northern Borneo. They have a very uncomfortable wedding ritual, according to which the use of bathroom is prohibited.

The Tidong people are known for their hospitality. They are warm and friendly people who usually earn their living by farming. Their traditional ceremonies revolve around magic, spirit worship, shamans, and other occult beliefs.

Most marriage ceremonies from all over the world focus on the well-being of the couple. During the ceremonies, various rituals are followed to ensure a happy married life. One such custom in the culture of Tidong people deals with fertility.

According to this custom, the bride and the groom are prohibited from using the restroom for three days after marriage. They can't go to the bathroom for anything. It is believed that this kind of abstinence is required to ensure fertility.

FAST FACT . . .

Bridesmaids were traditionally supposed to wear the same clothes as the bride to confuse evil spirits and robbers.

To make it a little easier and ensure that the couple don't cheat, the newly-weds are given as little food and water as possible. It is also believed that the hardship this couple faces during these three days prepares them for any kind of hardships that they might face during their married life.

FAST FACT . . .

The meaning of word "groom" in Old English is man. It comes from word "guma."

82. DATING RITUALS

Here's a bizarre tradition from Austria that will make you scrunch up your nose. It's a kind of dating ritual that was followed in the 19th century in Austria. Read on to find out how sweaty apple slices ended up being a measure of love.

Today, dating usually comprises of meals or a long walk on the beach. The idea behind it is that both people should be equally interested in spending time with each other.

The idea of love and marriage has evolved along with us. The customs and traditions surrounding the process of dating would surprise you. Austria had a particularly strange custom that it would follow.

A dance was organized for all the boys and girls of a particular age group. However, this was not your traditional Victorian dance. The women would saunter in with apple slices tucked under their armpits. When the music stopped playing, they would offer the sweat-soaked apple slice to the partner of their choice.

If he ate it and happened to like it, they would date!

FAST FACT . . .
You have maximum sweat glands on your soles and minimum on your back.

FAST FACT . . .
The yellowish underarm stains are caused due to the proteins and fatty acids present in sweat.

FAST FACT . . .
According to a tradition in ancient China, ladies danced with a stool hidden under their skirt. If the guy she was attracted to happened to cross her while dancing, she would remove the stool and offer him to sit.

83. SKY BURIAL

According to the Tibetan practice, the dead are not buried or burnt; instead, they are left out in the open for the vultures to feed on. While this practice may seem strange to most of us, there's a perfectly logical explanation behind it.

Tibetans believe that once the person is dead, his soul moves on, leaving the body behind. They see the body as nothing but a "discarded shell." So, instead of performing elaborate rituals around their deceased, they just leave it out in the open so that it disintegrates and goes back to nature.

But, this isn't the only reason behind this ritual. It was also a lot more practical to leave the dead out in the open. Tibet is a country with a very harsh climate. The land there is either solid rock or frozen. You can imagine how difficult digging in this topography would be! Graves were pretty much out of the question. Tibet also didn't have too much wood around to burn the dead bodies, which is why leaving the bodies out in the open was almost a necessity.

FAST FACT . . .
This Tibetan ritual is being followed for more than 2,300 years now.

FAST FACT . . .
The vultures who feed on dead bodies are considered to be sacred in Tibetan belief.

84. JUMPING THE BROOM

If you were to tell an African American to "jump the broom" with you, you'd effectively be asking them to marry you! This phrase means marriage for many African American communities. One can understand the "leap of faith" or even "tying the knot," but what could possibly be the origin of "jumping the broom?" Why would a couple jump over brooms to signify their eternal love and devotion to each other? There is a very interesting story behind it.

The tradition of jumping the broom originated in Ghana, West Africa. In the 18th century this region was ruled by the Asante of the Ashanti Confederacy. They were very neat and clean people who believed in keeping their streets spic and span. This is why the broom was a very important household item in those times.

Apart from its practical use, the broom was also used symbolically to remove evil spirits and sweep away past wrongs.

So when the time came for a couple to get married, the broom was waved over the couple's head to ward off the evil spirits. And sometimes the

FAST FACT . . .
The Wiccans and Gypsies have also taken to the tradition of jumping the broom.

Americans who were brought from Ghana to America, and the custom was soon picked up by other African Americans too.

broom was placed in front of the couple and they were asked to jump over it.

Jumping the broom, in such situations, signified that the wife is committing to the marriage and willing to keep a clean house. For the husband, it signified that he is taking his responsibility seriously.

While the practice faded away from Ghana, it was kept alive in the houses of the African-

85. JEWISH WEDDINGS

Every community seems to have some interesting customs associated with marriage. These customs have equally fascinating origins. In Jewish weddings, a thin glass wrapped in a napkin is smashed to the ground to solemnize the couple.

A number of utensils are used in a marriage ceremony. In ancient times, Jewish people used wine cups, which were also known as nuptial cups. After the nuptial vows were solemnized, the wine cup was smashed on the ground just in front of the groom's feet to declare that the ceremony has been satisfactorily completed.

The breaking of glass, according to Judaism, reminds everyone in this great moment of happiness not to forget the tragic destruction of the Temple of Jerusalem. It is a solemn moment, where Jewish people remember their roots. It is also believed that breaking the sacred cup gives out blessings for the newly wedded couple.

After breaking the glass, the bride and groom end their day-long fast, rest for a while, and meet the wedding guests.

FAST FACT . . .
It is customary for the couple to fast on their wedding day.

86. JUNE 21

June 21 is a happy day for many civilizations. No, it's not a national holiday. Yet, many traditions revolve around the longest day of the year. So what do people celebrate, and how?

In the northern hemisphere, the longest day of the year is called the summer solstice. In the southern hemisphere, it's the winter solstice. The word solstice comes from the Latin word "sol," meaning Sun, and "sistere," which means to stand still.

This day has been of importance since pre-Christian times. It has been a day of exceptions for many ancient civilizations. On this day, slaves were allowed to celebrate just like the elite class. There would be games and feasts for all.

According to Roman traditions, married women, who were otherwise not allowed to enter the temple of goddess Vesta, were allowed to worship in the temple all day. Goddess Vesta is regarded as the goddess of home and hearth.

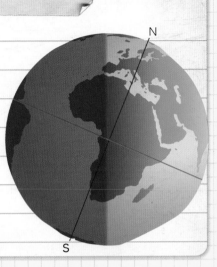

The Aztecs and Mayans noted this day and marked it for all important constructions. That is because on this day, the Sun is directly above the Tropic of Cancer, and observing the shadow on this day helped in making upright structures.

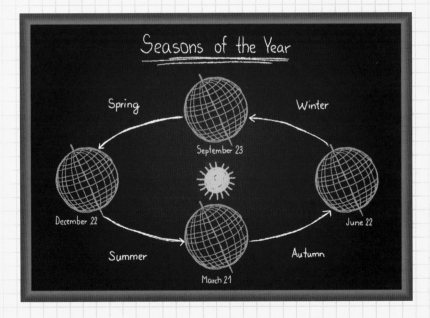

87. FUNERAL CUSTOMS

In ancient times, a lot of practices related to the dead originated only to please the spirits, who were believed to have caused the person's death. These rituals and rites differ across communities and regions, but a lot of our current practices stem from them.

One such custom was shutting the eyes of the dead, to close the window between the living and the dead. The tradition of covering the deceased with a cloth came from the Pagan belief that the soul of the dead escaped through the mouth.

Some cultures, though, took the fear a little too far. The English Saxons cut off the feet of their dead so that the corpse would be unable to walk. Some aborigine tribes even cut off the heads of the dead, thinking that the spirit would be too busy searching for this head to bother haunting the living.

FAST FACT . . .

In 19th century Europe, the dead were carried out of their house feet first, so that the spirit would not look back in the house and take another family member along with him.

88. SANTA CLAUS

The story of Santa Claus begins in 280 A.D., when St. Nicholas was born. He was a Christian priest from Greece who later became a bishop. He was very popular among the poor and needy. He would travel all around the country, distributing gifts at night when no one was looking.

How did St. Nicholas turn into the popular, red-coated, white-bearded Santa Claus? It so happened that over the years, people stopped worshipping St. Nicholas, and started looking at him as Father Christmas. When the tales of his popularity reached Europe, the Dutch mispronounced his name as "Sinter Klass." Soon, it was transformed to Santa Claus.

The current image of the plump old jolly man is actually the brain child of Coca-Cola

FAST FACT . . .
Prior to 1931, Santa Claus was depicted as many things, ranging from a tall, thin man to a pesky little elf!

to boost their sales. Santa Claus has been featuring in Coca-Cola ads since the 1920s.

Now you know that the only reason Santa wears red is because red is the brand color for Coca Cola!

89. LABOR DAY

On this day, Americans celebrate the social and economic achievements of their workers. It all began during the era in which workers were exploited – they were made to work long hours and not paid proper wages. The conditions were harsh.

It was Peter McGuire, a carpenter, who brought the change. He came up with the idea of Labor Day in 1872. Protesting against the long working hours and harsh working environment, Peter McGuire convinced around 100,000 laborers to go on strike. After spending a decade fighting for Labor Rights, in 1882, 10,000 workers walked on the first Labor Day parade. The conditions of laborers have changed since then, and in 1894, Congress declared Labor Day a national holiday.

LABOR DAY

90. WOMEN'S MONTH

That's right, there's an entire month dedicated to the contributions of the "gentler sex" toward their history, culture, and society. This month was actually started at a local school event in California. In 1987, the USA started recognizing March as Women's History Month.

It began as a week-long celebration when presentations were given in around a dozen schools and many students participated in an essay writing contest on the topic "Real Women." In 1980, the week of March 8 was declared as the Women's History Week by President Jimmy Carter. Eventually, the whole month of March was called the Women's History Month. Every year, the theme of this month differs.

91. HALLOWEEN

Most of us have gone trick-or-treating during Halloween. You may also know that this festival is associated with pumpkin heads, witches, and all things spooky. But you probably didn't know that this scary, yet playful festival originated from the Celtic Festival called "Samhain."

In the ancient festival of Samhain, people would light fires and wear costumes to ward off roaming ghosts. In the eighth century, Pope Gregory III decided that November 1 would be All Saints Day, to honor all the martyrs and saints. This day incorporated some of the Samhanian traditions. The evening before All Saints Day came to be known as All Hallow's Eve, and this soon came to be pronounced as Halloween.

FAST FACT . . .

The Irish began the tradition of carving pumpkins, by carving out turnips on Halloween to ward off evil spirits. However, as the tradition traveled across the globe to the USA, pumpkins proved easier to carve.

92. FLU PANDEMIC

There was a time in history when 500 million people were sneezing simultaneously! Because of its size, this flu was termed a pandemic, which means that it affected the entire world. The pandemic lasted from 1918 to 1919.

Slowly, people started becoming aware that the world was falling prey to this flu. The death toll started rising, and by the time the pandemic receded, it was believed that around 20-50 million people had been killed by it.

The first wave of Spanish Flu, as it was known, hit Europe in 1918 at the end of World War I. People started falling ill and experienced typical symptoms of the flu, such as fever and chills, which lasted for several days. This slowly started spreading from Europe to USA and parts of Asia.

93. SLAVERY

We're all aware of the existence of slavery on American plantations in the 17th, 18th, and 19th centuries. Most of the slaves were ill-treated, and had no choice in their profession, as the son of a slave was forced to replace his father.
This treatment led to civil unrest and war, until the slaves gained their freedom in 1865, when slavery was abolished.

Slavery began in the USA with the arrival of the first African slaves in 1619. They were brought to North America to work in tobacco plantations. Slowly, their population grew. Slavery was rampant in the 17th and 18th centuries. In the 19th century, the great American Civil War took place, where the slaves demanded freedom. Four million slaves were freed during the period of Reconstruction from 1865 to 1877.

94. MAYFLOWER

The Mayflower is a ship that crossed the Atlantic Ocean through a severe storm in 1620. Because the passengers managed to survive such adverse conditions, it was believed that the hand of God was protecting them, and so they were called pilgrims.

The Mayflower set off from Plymouth, England, in 1602. It so happened that Mayflower was actually a merchant ship. It was supposed to just carry wine and dry goods. But a neighboring boat called Speedwell, which had left along with Mayflower, started leaking. This is why all of the 102 passengers of Speedwell were transferred to Mayflower.

A lot of the people on the ship were Protestant Separatists, who wanted to establish a new Church in the New World. This also contributed to why they came to be known as pilgrims.

96. WASHINGTON DC

You probably know that Washington DC is home to the White House and the capital of the USA, but have you ever wondered if there's any connection between George Washington, and the city? If you have, you're absolutely right!

stating that the site chosen by George Washington would be the capital of the USA. And so it was!

Washington DC is situated on the north bank of Potomac River and is home to the White House, the Supreme Court, and the Capitol Building. Though George Washington overlooked the entire construction of the White House, he never really stayed there.

The crowning of Washington DC as a capital happened on July 16, 1790. Thomas Jefferson, Alexander Hamilton, and James Madison signed an agreement

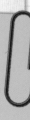

FAST FACT . . .

It has been estimated that native American tribes first settled in Washington 4,000 years ago.

95. NEW YORK

We're all aware of the concrete jungle that is now New York, but it wasn't always New York. Enjoy this blast from the past as we introduce you to the history of New York.

It all began in 1624 when the Dutch first settled on the coast of the Hudson River. Two years later, on Manhattan Island, they developed a colony and called it New Amsterdam. Four decades later the English came over and took control. That is when they renamed this place as New York.

FAST FACT . . .

New York played a very important role in the American Revolution.

FAST FACT . . .

Millions of immigrants came through Ellis Island on their journey to New York to become US citizens between 1892 and 1954.

97. FLORIDA

This Sunshine State joined the Union as the 27th State in 1845. There's a story behind the origin of its name, though. The name was not randomly picked; it was discovered by Spanish explorer Juan Ponce de Leon.

their vacations here because of its scenic, flowery beauty.

As this place was discovered by a Spanish explorer, the story has a Spanish flavor to it.

Explorer Juan Ponce de Leon was the governor of Bimini and Florida under the King of Spain.

Florida lies in the south-eastern part of the USA. It is the eighth most densely populated state, and people just love to spend

FAST FACT . . .
Saint Augustine in northern Florida is the oldest European settlement in North America.

However, one day, he was replaced by Columbus' son. Juan was quite hurt by this loss of honor. So he set off on the first European expedition in the year 1513. When he came across this state, he decided to call it Florida after the Spanish festival "Pascua Florida" which means "Feast of Flowers." And that's how the wonderful state of Florida got its name!

FAST FACT . . .
The longest river sailboat race is conducted in Florida. It is called the "Annual Mug Race."

CURRENCY

HERBERT HOOVERS

SOFT GOLD

BARTER SYSTEM

SKIRT LENGTH INDEX

FUR TAX

PAPER MONEY

COINS

ECONOMICS

COPPER COINS

THE GREAT DEPRESSION

98. PAPER MONEY

We all know that our ancient times – the times of kingdoms and rulers – are filled with clinking gold, silver, and bronze coins. When did the fashion of paper money break in? Who set this convenient trend? Let's find out.

It all began in the Tang dynasty which was prevalent in the seventh century. For a while people were satisfied with their conventional, age-old copper coins, but gradually they grew tired of carrying the heavy load.

In cases of large transactions, lots of manpower was required to carry the bundles of coins. That was when merchants began depositing "certificates" which were worth a certain amount of money.

FAST FACT . . .
Sweden issued its first
currency notes in 1661.

These certificates were the
ancestors of our currency notes.
Since they were so much lighter
to carry than the chunky copper
coins, they were also called
"flying money." But the use
of this "flying money" wasn't
widespread in those times.
It was used only in the case of
transactions involving
huge amounts.

FAST FACT . . .
Copper coins finally gave
way to paper money when
there was a shortage
of copper.

99. FUR AS MONEY

Money as we know it today underwent a lot of transformation. Different regions developed different monetary forms before it finally found its way into our bank accounts. One of these forms was animal fur. It was used widely in Siberia in the 1600s, when hunters and trappers started making their way into this freezing land.

The Russian fur trade is known to be as intense as the Gold Rush in California. It all began when Russians landed in Siberia in the 1600s and realized that the natives owned beautiful and exquisite furs. Slowly, more Russians started pouring into this land and thus began the world's historical fur trade.

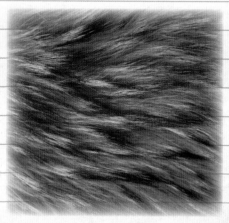

FAST FACT . . .

People who refused to pay "yasak" were attacked and their property was raided by local goons.

This trade played a very important role in the development of Siberia. As people from all over North America poured in to buy fur, money started entering Siberia. In those times, fur even came to be called "soft gold."

By the 17th century, this trade had become so prevalent that the government decided to impose taxes that were payable only in terms of fur. This made sure that a certain amount of fur stayed in the country. The tax came to be known as "yasak," and every male citizen above the age of 18 years was supposed to pay it.

FAST FACT . . .
The furs from Russian America were usually sold in China.

100. SKIRT LENGTH INDEX

Did you know that there's something called the Skirt Length Index and that it's linked to the economy of the country? It has proven to be quite reliable in the past too!

The birth of the economic index called the "Skirt Length Index" (SLI) took place 86 years ago when American Economist George Taylor made a very amusing observation – women raised their hemlines to show off their silk stockings when the economy was good, and hid themselves and their old battered stockings under long skirts when the economy suffered.

When unemployment in the UK was high in the 1980s, skirts began to grow longer and longer. Between 1984 and 1988, with the advent of the cell phone, skirts began to grow shorter once again.

And when the stock market crashed between 1989 to 1992, skirts grew longer once again! Though the rationale behind

this theory may not hold true today, studies conducted in 2012 have shown that the theory itself still holds true! A careful study of popular fashion sported by the likes of Victoria Beckham has shown that they wore longer skirts and dresses during the global recession in 2008.

Though there might be some truth to this theory, the next time you catch yourself observing the length of a woman's skirt, perhaps double checking it against a newspaper would be a good idea. Who knows, you might just be able to find the rationale behind the relation!

101. AMERICAN ECONOMY IN 1920

America's economy, which was whimpering in 1919, took a U-turn and started growing robustly in the 1920s, thanks to Commerce Secretary Herbert Hoover's strategy that convinced big industries to raise the wages of the workers.

This brought about a big change in the economy of America and it started growing manifold. The changes that this economy brought with it were huge. It was also termed "mass culture." The Americans now had ample money to spend, and consumerism grew – although many people were not comfortable with this huge shift. This newfound wealth was short-lived, though, because the Great Depression hit the country in 1929, with devastating effects.

FAST FACT . . .

Herbert Hoover later became President in 1929. He was defeated in 1932, though, and Franklin Roosevelt took over. However, a lot of the economic reforms that Hoover introduced laid the groundwork for Franklin's policies.

INDEX

A

Africa 13, 16, 73
African Americans 109, 164-5
agriculture 17, 30, 81
Allied forces 123
America 22-3, 102, 109, 144, 165, 188, 192
American troops 104-5, 128
Americans 110-11, 165, 192
ancestors 9, 12, 20, 66-7, 187
ancient civilizations 4, 20, 29, 31, 33, 35, 37, 39, 41, 43, 45, 47-9, 51, 53-5, 57
Ancient Egypt 20, 38, 40, 156
Ancient Egyptians 20, 41, 54
animals 13-14, 24, 40, 54, 66, 70, 76, 139
anthropologists 66, 73
Anthropology 4, 63, 65, 67, 69, 71, 73, 75, 77, 79, 81, 83, 85, 87, 89
archeologists 18, 20, 54, 70
Austria 113, 118, 160
Aztecs 48-9, 169

B

barter system 84
black codes 108-9
Black Death 154
bombs 116
Bronze Age 16-17, 50
burial 70, 162
Byzantine Empire 130

C

Carthage 96
cavemen 47
ceremonies 147, 157-8, 166
children 32, 42, 48, 77, 80, 107, 116, 121, 156
Chinese 46, 146, 148
Christians 94-5
civil war 108, 110
civilizations 30, 42, 44, 50, 52, 64, 156, 168
Cleopatra 34-5
Colosseum 60-1
communists 124, 128-9
communities 74, 76, 166, 170
country 5, 33, 92-3, 102, 106, 116, 146, 154, 162, 171, 189-90, 192

D

D-Day 123
dictatorship 92-3, 122
dynasties 100-1

E

Earth 5, 12, 17-18, 59, 100-1
Economics 4, 185, 187, 189, 191
education 48-9, 88, 122
Egypt 34-5, 37, 50, 54
Egyptian culture 35, 40
Egyptians 20-1, 36, 38, 40, 54-5, 69
Elizabeth Cady Stanton 106-7
Emperor Qin Shin Huang 100
Europe 154, 171, 176
evil spirits 164, 174
extinction 18-19

F

FBI (Federal Bureau of Investigation) 126
feudal lords 82, 97
forces, anti-Communist coalition 128
French Revolution 97

G

Genoa 98
Georgia 104-5
Germany 112, 115, 122
graves 68, 162
Great Wall of China 100-1
guerillas 102-3

H

Hadza tribe 45
Harbor, Pearl 114-15
Hiroshima 116
history 4, 7, 9, 11, 13, 15-17, 19, 21, 23, 25, 27, 35, 104, 106, 128-9
Hitler, Adolf 118, 120, 122
Holocaust 120-1
human beings 12, 18, 24
humans 10, 12-13, 15, 26, 78
hunting 12-14, 16, 23-4, 45, 73, 76, 78
    hunter-gatherers 73-4, 76
    nomadic hunters 22

I

Indonesia 18
Indus Valley Civilization 50-1
Industrial Revolution 86, 88
Iron Age 16-17

J

Japan 112, 114-16, 146, 150
Jerusalem 94-5, 166
Jews 94-5, 120-1

K

kings 35, 38, 82, 93

L

Labor Day 172
laborers 172
language 24, 45, 47-8, 54
    modern languages 45-6
Leon 182
Lucretia Mott 106

M

Manchuria 114
marriage 156-8, 160, 164-6
Mayans 42-4, 169
McGuire, Peter 172
Mesopotamia 20, 30-1, 50, 52, 56
Middle Ages 68, 82-3, 144
Minh, Chi 128
Mississippi 108-9
monks 150-1
mummies 38, 69
Muslims 94

N

Nagasaki 116
Native Americans 70
Nazis 120-2
Neanderthal 68-9
Neolithic Era 14, 17
Nixon, Richard 126-7

O

Oklahoma 104-5
Old Stone Age 14, 16

P

Paleolithic Era 14, 16
peasants 82-3
Pharaohs 36-8
placebo effect 138-9
Politics 4, 31, 91, 93, 95, 97, 99, 101, 103, 105, 107, 109, 111, 113, 115
Polo, Marco 98-9
priests 31, 48, 56, 59, 71
prison 98-9, 118
professions 70, 78, 81, 177

psychology 4, 72, 133, 135-7, 139, 141
Ptolemaic dynasty 34-5
Punic Wars 96

R

religions 72, 95
rituals 31, 43, 57, 68-9, 76, 146, 148, 150, 157-8, 160, 162, 170
Romans 46, 96, 153
Russia 112, 114
Russians 188

S

scientists 18, 26-7, 66, 68, 154
serfs 82
Siberia 188-9
slaves 82, 121, 153, 168, 177
societies 13, 24, 30, 51, 70, 73-4, 76-8, 80-2, 86, 88, 106, 152, 173
Sociology 4, 143, 145, 147, 149, 151, 153, 155, 157, 159, 161, 163, 165, 167, 169
Soviet Union 124-5, 128-9
Spartans 32-3
sports 60, 144-5
Stone Age 12-17, 24, 26, 64, 144
Study of Politics 93, 95, 97, 99, 101, 103, 105, 107, 109, 111, 113, 115, 117, 119, 121
Sumerians 31, 52-3

T

taxes 95, 189
temple 31, 58-9, 168
Tibet 162
tradition 31, 135, 144, 160-1, 170, 174

U

USA 104, 108, 112, 114-15, 124, 128-9, 139, 173-4, 176-7, 179, 182

V

Vietnam War 124, 128-9

W

war 5, 32, 64, 96, 98, 102, 110-13, 115, 123-4, 177
warfare 49, 102-3
    guerilla 102-3, 131
women 13, 65, 106-7, 109, 161, 190
world 4, 7, 9, 11-13, 15, 17, 19, 21, 30-1, 45, 50, 92, 100, 157, 176
World War 112-13, 120, 176
World War II 113, 116, 120, 122-3, 125